To the artists and writers who embody *The Right to Hope* and to those whose lives they touch, South Africa welcomes you with a warm embrace. We know that you will find with us a natural home in a land where the barren earth of bitter division, oppression and hatred is being transformed each day into a soil rich with seeds of hope, peace and reconciliation. In your celebration of the uniqueness and creativity of so many human cultures, of the victory of truth and justice over inhumanity and deceit, we share with you a vision of a better world whose creation is the responsibility of each and every one of us. It can be accomplished only by our coming together in a spirit of goodwill, with tolerance, understanding and clear resolve.

We gladly offer *The Right to Hope* a place from which to begin its global journey as we commemorate the 50th anniversary of the United Nations. This anniversary gives each of us cause to reflect on the past and to recommit ourselves to a future where global co-operation and human well-being are more than just distant ideals. The bonds between South Africa and this project are close; fostering the diversity of our cultural expression is integral in our move towards securing the individual's right to political and social equality. From a country which knows all too well how difficult such journeys can be – but from one where the quiet miracle of humanity's interdependence has been witnessed by the whole world – we wish you Godspeed.

Mandela

NELSON MANDELA

The Right to Hope

Global Problems, Global Visions

Creative Responses to our World in Need

The Right to Hope Trust is grateful for the kind support of DANIDA

Joy Harjo's 'Eagle Poem' is from *In Mad Love and War*,
Wesleyan University Press, 1990,
by permission of University Press of New England

First published in the UK in 1995
by Earthscan Publications Limited

Copyright © *The Right to Hope Trust,* 1995

All rights reserved

A catalogue record for this book is available from the British Library

ISBN 1 85383 309 6

Printed and bound in Great Britain by
BPC Paulton Books Limited
A member of
The British Printing Company

Cover and text designed by Dominic Banner
Cover illustration: Reconciliation by Nicholas Mukomberanna, Zimbabwe

For a full list of publications please contact:

Earthscan Publications Limited
120 Pentonville Road
London N1 9JN
Tel: 44 (0)171 278 0433
Fax: 44 (0)171 278 1142

Earthscan is an editorially independent subsidiary of Kogan Page Limited and publishes in association with WWF-UK and the International Institute for Environment and Development.

Contents

The Artists and Their Work — vi
Foreword by Njabulo Ndebele — vii
Preface — ix
Introduction Catherine Thick — xi

Chapter 1	**Nothing Short of a Miracle** *Archbishop Desmond Tutu*	1
Chapter 2	**Why Stop Now?** *Susan George*	5
Chapter 3	**Bottlenecks of Development** *Wangari Maathai*	9
Chapter 4	**Bringing the World to Bear: Media, Culture and Development** *Adrian Cleasby*	17
Chapter 5	**Population and Empowerment** *Nafis Sadik*	25
Chapter 6	**Satyagraha** *Anil Agarwal*	31
Chapter 7	**Idealism in Practice: Comprehending the Incomprehensible** *Mary Midgley*	39
Chapter 8	**Bridging Civilisations** *Saad Eddin Ibrahim*	45
Chapter 9	**Monocultures, Monopolies and the Masculinisation of Knowledge** *Vandana Shiva*	53
Chapter 10	**The Cultural Dimensions of Development** *Javier Perez de Cuellar*	61
Chapter 11	**Governance in our Global Neighbourhood** *Shridath Ramphal*	65
Chapter 12	**The Global and the Local: Planting the Seeds of Hope** *Alicia Barcena*	69
Chapter 13	**Visions for the Future** *Phil Lane*	75

About the Artists — 83
About the Authors — 91

The Artists and Their Work

Argentina   Anahi Caceres
Archaeology of the Third Millenium
Australia and Chile   Judy Watson and Gonzalo Mella
A Brief History of Colonisation
Bangladesh   Hamiduzzaman Khan
Trees Live then Humankind Will Survive
Brazil   Siron Franco
Flesh and Furs
Canada   Angus Cockney Kaanerk
Collaboration
Chile and Mexico   Celia Martner Peyrelongue
Legend
China   Zeng Shanqing and Yang Yanping
Pray for Generations to Come
Colombia   Maria Teresa Cano
Tendido
Cote d'Ivoire   Youssouf Bath
The Disaster: Search for Hope
Cuba   Santiago Rodriguez Olazabal
A Dead Man Leaves Behind all his Possesions
Dominican Repubilc   Tony Capellan
Small Hope
Egypt   Gazbia Sirry
Hope
Estonia   Ivo Lill
Aspiration
Ethiopia   Zerihun Yetmgeta
Magic Art
Finland   Osmo Rauhala
Cosmic Memory
Germany and Ghana   Owusu Ankomah
Sympathy
Ghana and Nigeria   El Anatsui
Unfolding the Scroll of History
Guatemala   Efrain Recinos
Construction of the Future
Haiti and USA   Marilene Phipps
Prayer House
India   Vivan Sundaram
Gun Carriage
Indonesia   Ansupati
Tribute to Bosnia-Herzegovina
Iran and Hungary   Gizella Varga Sinai
Forgotten Paradise
Japan   Kimio Tsuchiya
Moon
Jordan   Khalid Khreis
Change

Kenya   Steve Ngige
Portrait of Love
Korea   Duck-Hyun Cho
Light of Hope
Malaysia   Ariffin Mohd Ismail
Meeting Point
Mali   Groupe Bogolan Kasobane
The Long March
Martinique   Victor Anicet
Tray
Mexico   Nestor Quinones
Tree of LIfe
Namibia   Joe Madisia
Tree of Unity
Nigeria   Nike Olaniyi Davies
The Tree of Life
Palestine and UK   Laila Shawa
Children of War, Children of Peace
Paraguay   Monica Gonzalez and Osvaldo Salerno
Wash and Wear
Peru   Movimiento Manuela Ramos
Restaurant and Market
Sierra Leone   Louise Metzger
Hope
Slovenia   Marko Pogacnik
Cosmogramme
South Africa   Willem Boshoff
Bottled Hope
Sudan   Rashid Diab
Diary of an Immigrant
Swaziland   Johan Mhlanga
Two People and a Fish
Tibet   Gongkar Gyatso
Lotus
Turkey   Handan Borutecene
Cosmic Envelopes
Ukraine   Alexander Borodie
Joining the Past and the Present
United Kingdom   One World Quilt Group
One World Quilt
Uruguay   Rimer Cardillo
Lost Forest Reliquaries
Venezuela   Ricardo Benaim
Homage to the Three Kingdoms
Vietnam   Buu Chi
Requiem
Zimbabwe   Gladman Zinyeka
Homage to Refugees

FOREWORD

Njabulo Ndebele

Recently I learned of the formation of a new organisation in The Netherlands with the acronym IZA. This organisation is the result of reassessment by the vast anti-apartheid movement in Europe and Scandinavia of their relationship with South Africa and Southern Africa after the demise of apartheid and the arrival of democracy. Diverse peoples all over the world had willingly given of themselves in various ways to support the South African struggle for liberation. It was inevitable that deep feelings for South Africa and concern over its future would develop. It became clear that it would not be enough to end apartheid, it would also be essential to ensure the survival and sustainability of the new democracy and the region in which it is located. So, there has been a new coming together in the anti-apartheid movement; an emergence of new visions; the redefining of goals and new commitments.

That is why the acronym IZA (Instituut voor Zuidelijk Afrika, Dutch for Institute for Southern Africa) struck me immediately. It carried an additional meaning which the founders of the institute were most probably not aware of. In the Zulu language iza means 'come' with the attendant connotation of 'coming together'. What a remarkable coincidence! And so it is that South Africans have to reconfigure their relationships with one another as well as with the rest of the world. They are working to discover commonalities on the basis of which they can come together as a people. At the same time, they have to come together with the world community. *The Right to Hope* project reverberates with similar meanings. The peoples of the world must learn to break old barriers, build new relationships, define new common commitments, establish new loyalties, and experience the world in new ways. Coming together.

The decision to launch *The Right to Hope* in South Africa is fraught with symbolism. Firstly, South Africa currently embodies the meaning of fresh beginnings. Secondly, the exhibition will coincide with the 50th anniversary of the founding of the United Nations. In this connection, major demographic shifts are underway globally, resulting in the countries of the South moving rapidly into the centre of world events. It is expected consequently that there will be major shifts of orientation and focus in the United Nations. The attempt of *The Right to Hope* project to approach the process of reorientation through the dimension of art, and its inherent tendency towards coherence, suggests that not only are there other vital ways of experiencing and responding to our world, but also that there are other uses to which science and technology can be put to deal more effectively and more creatively with mass poverty, illiteracy, unemployment, and environmental degradation. Fresh beginnings and reorientations!

Everywhere in South Africa today, there is evidence of a mass reawakening as many people, previously denied opportunities, are now entering various aspects of public life. Now on the pavements of South Africa's towns and cities are countless numbers of people trading; hundreds of thousands of workers throughout the country are testing out their rights on the factory floor; black business peoples are increasing their stake in the corporate world day by day. Previously inaccessible professions are literally being invaded. People are entering professions such as aviation, tourism, computing, finances, advertising. They have entered parliament; are becoming diplomats; are members of various kinds of statutory councils which many never knew even existed. The landless are occupying unused land. New artists, musicians, photographers, TV presenters, film makers, are emerging every day. It is a slow revolution with increasing pervasiveness; the meaning of freedom taking shape slowly but purposefully.

What is happening is that people are discovering their potential as individuals. At the same time, the horizons of the world around them are expanding constantly. That is to say, the growth of personal awareness occurs simultaneously with the awareness of an expanding local, national, and international environment. The on-going reconfiguration of the national environment and the total nature of that process gives South Africans the rare opportunity of experiencing coherence in their daily lives. They have the opportunity to see and appreciate the vital connection between the individual and the community; between the rural and the urban; between the social and the natural environments.

There is a potential, therefore, for a new sense of public awareness. By the same token there is among the community of nations, the real potential for a new sense of international awareness. The concept of a global village is increasingly a reality, particularly as a result of communication and information technology. At the same time, people the world over are increasingly aware of what threatens human survival: AIDS, chemical weapons, nuclear and other kinds of toxic waste, deforestation, and other similar threats.

Promoting international awareness and cooperation does not come easy. These are matters to be worked at. After all, the human environment in South Africa is still polluted by the past. For example, the residential areas are still largely segregated. It requires a great deal of patience and tolerance to live with what you had sought to change because the process of change is a long one. But it is precisely in the interim that the ethical sense is sharpened and moral endurance developed.

The Right to Hope is an important building block in a necessary process that may take some time to reach fruition. But the journey towards the objective of peace is as important as the objective itself. The artists of the world will enable us not only to understand more, but also to have the capacity to be patient at the same time that we double our efforts.

P REFACE

The Right to Hope brings together artists, writers, leaders, scholars and organisations from around the world who are dedicated to helping realise a better world.

This book is part of the international One World Art *Right to Hope* project which also includes a television series, a travelling exhibition, educational materials, and a charitable Trust. The project commemorates the 50th anniversaries of the United Nations and UNESCO (the UN's Educational, Scientific and Cultural Organisation) in 1995 and 1996 respectively: anniversaries that are reminders of hope for a new order of peace, equity, and environmental security.

Complementing the images and statements of 48 very diverse artists, the essays cover a broad range of disciplines such as global governance, religion, media, science, economics, and philosophy. Although the essays vary in their perspective and content, there is an overriding message; in a time of environmental destruction and entrenched poverty, we need to emphasise the importance of social, cultural and spiritual values in national, institutional and global affairs if humanity is to live together sustainably on planet earth. Securing a better world cannot be left to treaties, economics and technology alone; our efforts must be founded on human initiative, political will and creative spirit.

Culture is not something separate from the development debate; culture is us, it is who we are and the visions we have of the world. The original works depicted here show art as a positive force for education and change; they have all been especially created in response to the theme of 'one world', to our world in need. Beside the images of their work, the accompanying statements by the artists explain the beliefs and rationale behind their work.

The creation of some of these artworks is featured in the One World Art *Right to Hope* television series produced by the One World Group of Broadcasters. The Group invited broadcasters from around the world to take part in this evocative series; it is a unique contribution toward demonstrating both the power of culture to foster cross-cultural communication and understanding, and the ability of art to promote values for human survival and peace. The programmes encompass the celebration of human creativity, appreciation of traditional and indigenous cultures, environmental protection and social justice, and articulate them to a broad audience. The most rewarding and astonishing aspect of the series is the overwhelming variety of technique, motivation and style, a vivid expression of human aspirations, and a very direct statement of both the difference and commonality of human experience.

Most of the works illustrated in this book are also included in an exhibition, opened in South Africa in September of 1995, which tours globally for two years to countries including Egypt, Germany, India, Australia, Chile and the United States. The exhibition consists of paintings, sculpture and installations, showing the difference in the context and origin of art forms worldwide. The exhibition shows that the arts of Asia, Africa and Latin America are thriving, and provides an inspirational site of communication and debate as the artists express their concerns and aspirations for the future. South Africa was invited to host the exhibition as the country represents so well the hopes and difficulties addressed by the project, a sentiment expressed beautifully by President Mandela at the beginning of the book. Indeed, the long-term work of the project stems from South Africa where *The Right to Hope Trust* was established in 1995.

A major priority of the Trust is educational, centred on the video education pack developed by One World Support UK and the Trust. The pack consists of a booklet and laminated sheets along with a video of ten of the programmes featured in the television series. The pack takes a lead from the issues the artists themselves raise, along with country profiles, and information on their cultural backgrounds, and pressing social and environmental issues. The films and pack are therefore a resource for the humanities as well as art education.

The main strength of the pack is to show how art can counteract the often negative assumptions and prejudices held about the less powerful or so called 'developing' nations. As the exhibition tours the world, further material accumulates as artists, community groups, schools, non-governmental organisations and institutions, in each host country, respond to the presence of *The Right to Hope*. The Trust will then adapt, integrate, and disseminate these materials, collaborating with other agencies within and beyond South Africa.

Besides its commitment to development, educational, cultural and human rights issues both locally and internationally, the Trust will help raise awareness around the world of the objectives underlying *The Right to Hope*. The project was founded on the belief that it is within the power of each of us to help bring about a better world. Encouraging public participation in seeking more responsible and humane policies by governments, institutions and multinationals is pivotal to the Trust's activities.

In the Foreword, Professor Ndebele writes of a 'coming together'. *The Right to Hope* is a communion of diverse cultures. It is a vehicle for a unique and united expression which is gathering global momentum. More than this, the project embodies a message: art, thought and creative inspiration can spur positive action for change in a world where future is threatened. We are the agents of change, all of us, linked by our mutual dependence. The artists, audiences, thinkers, agencies, teachers and learners who have come together through this project foster that change with dignity, humanity, tolerance and hope.

The One World Art *Right to Hope* project has been made possible by the collaboration and support of organisations and individuals around the world. The following are due particular acknowledgement: the participating artists and authors; UNESCO and the United Nations; James Porter, former Director of the Commonwealth Institute; Ritchie Cogan, Director of the One World Group of Broadcasters; Karl Mertes of WDR in Cologne, Executive Producer of the television series; Paddy Coulter, Director of the International Broadcasting Trust; Liz Rowlands, Coordinator of One World Support UK; the International Institute for Environment and Development; and all those in South Africa who helped realise the exhibition and Trust.

Introduction

Culture and Change: An Artist's Perspective

There is a timeless language to art. Despite enormous differences in practice, art is found in every human grouping, past and present, where the activity or artefact is in a realm outside the everyday. Artists share concerns, beliefs and visions which transcend place, time, or medium of expression.

In many societies, human beings are considered to be the heart or conscience of the universe; art is seen as one of the most magnificent and valuable things human beings can create where it represents, or seeks to represent, the spirit. For most artists, the world has a moral dimension, meaning there are overriding issues of integrity, dignity and responsibility; they describe values for human survival and peace. This is true for many of us, but artists have the ability to express these issues so powerfully that they can influence a very wide audience.

Artists are drawn to the areas where great behavioural changes are occurring. As a painter, I have long sought to identify underlying beliefs upon which to work and have reached the following conclusions. First of all, our inhumanity to nature is a reflection of man's inhumanity to man, where poverty is accepted as an aspect of the existing economic order; secondly, the condition of humanity is set on a course towards material security and spiritual advancement, and the achievements of our species deserve celebration; thirdly, mistakes are part of progress and the qualities that make our species distinct – our intellect and creativity – increasingly enable us to conceptualise the outcome of our actions if we have the courage and honesty to ask the right questions. And finally, of greatest importance, the basis of a just world order must be the universal respect for human rights, based on respect for the miracle of the Universe, of Nature, for our very existence.

The sustainability of our environment becomes more fragile as we remove ourselves from the natural order. New technology may allow us to radically alter the basic biological laws that limit a species' expansion but we must respect the habitat from which we emerged. We still have much to learn about nature and we still rely upon the earth's equanimity, the certainty that it will provide for us. We are becoming estranged from the very reality, and the very mystery, with which we need to achieve a close relationship, and for which we need to kindle a sense of awe and reverence. This makes our crisis a spiritual one as well. And we should imagine a spiritual dimension becoming more critical to our survival as a species. This global vulnerability is the challenge that could pull our species to a new level, to a new 'humanism'.

Hope is the engine of change. The goal of securing peace, equity and environmental security cannot just be left to treaties, multilateral agencies, or to economics. To succeed, it must be founded on human initiative and creativity. Beside scientists, philosophers, political and religious leaders, artists too have a role as critics and prophets of their societies. Art conveys that for each of us there are intimations of truth, beauty and goodness which are irreducible, and which motivate us to rise above the mundane demands of life. Beauty and tragedy in art testify to the potential of the human spirit and creativity to transcend and transform material conditions. It is belief in this potential that founded *The Right to Hope* project.

The creation of a new order depends more than anything on the aspirations and hard work of ordinary individuals. Enlightened public opinion could galvanise governments to enact difficult proposals on such issues as disarmament, international debt and the environment. Together, perhaps as yet unrealised, we hold the power. Art is necessary here as a vehicle for hope, inspiration and education. Artists can help us rediscover the values too often marginalised in contemporary life – imaginative and spiritual values. Art has the power to communicate the continuum of life, the thread that links the past, present and future. It has the power to demonstrate, along with other disciplines such as history, sociology and economics, that to progress society needs to recognise both what has worked and what has failed in the past, and to use that knowledge to identify the right way forward.

There are signs that we are reaching a time of crisis. The elements of the crisis we face are invisible, global, and potentially lethal. The forces generated by our techno-scientific economy are now great enough to destroy the planet. Human societies themselves are in danger of destruction as we undermine our cultural and social inheritance. The factors igniting conflict between cultures are increasing. Our world risks both explosion and implosion. It must change to survive.

History is littered with examples of civilisations which collapsed because they failed to adapt. The purpose of all governments should be the promotion of the common good of the people. But governments frequently fail to hold human well-being as an objective; it becomes displaced with a desire for power or the overriding belief in a political ideology at the expense of all else, usually resulting in considerable human suffering. Governments and citizens in all parts of the world must address these contradictions.

We are still largely governed by the structures and doctrines of an order whose roots can be traced through layers of competition and exploitation. We are witnessing the continuation of centuries of economic and cultural destruction of societies, especially of indigenous peoples and their habitats. To use the word genocide is not too strong – a loss of land and language, of community and theology. A system of exploitation exists in which vested interests prevail; a trade of guns, debt, cheap labour and poverty. Free market forces can bring benefits, but it is close to a universal truth that capitalism, now embraced eagerly by leaders in most countries, stifles the spirit.

Race and class distinctions are part of the control mechanism that keeps labour forces within condoned social and political bounds. But racism is not confined as an issue from black to white, it exists both within and between nations. Social distinctions have become a driving force of the body politic – we have a duty to seek a higher order of public ethic. As Vaclav Havel, President of the Czech Republic, when speaking of freedom and racism in abusive regimes, puts it:

> *It is not hard to demonstrate that all the main threats confronting the world today, from atomic war and ecological disaster to a catastrophic collapse of society and civilisation ... have hidden deep within them a single root cause: the imperceptible transformation of what was originally a humble message into an arrogant one ... Having learned from all this, we should fight together against arrogant words ... obviously this is not just a linguistic task. Responsibility for and towards words is a task which is intrinsically ethical.*

We are faced with a different cold war; a war of the North against the South, reflected through the terms 'First World' and 'Third World'. Language is equally dehumanising when it comes to developmental issues. Countries with low GNP (Gross National Product) are referred to, officially and unofficially, as underdeveloped or developing. Residents of the developing countries are the Poor, the Hungry, the Other. They are, most degradingly, seen only as Victims. One can pity victims and offer charity. But with the mounting racism both within and between nations, it becomes harder for society to see victims as equals, to value their cultures, and to accommodate them. But the capacity

of people to maintain their traditional values in the face of the onslaught from market economics is not confined to the South alone.

Most models of development ignore indigenous or traditional modes of relating to the world, and promote free market values. A worldwide simplification of languages and cultures is a form of deprivation: as monoculture spreads, viable alternatives to the industrial growth society are eroded. As a result, our capacity to meet an increasingly difficult future with creative responses has been considerably impoverished. We need to listen to the disadvantaged or oppressed before deciding what development consists of; not only must they have a large say in the solutions, but they already contain within themselves large parts of the solutions. Forty years of 'development' has demonstrated beyond doubt that unless communities are authors of change, it does not work. Successful models of development integrate social, physical and economic conditions on a local level, and promote self-sufficiency.

Development should not be a process of intervention; it should be a process of empowerment while acknowledging our interdependence. Awareness of our interdependence could produce a new concept of self-interest; we must show that defending the interests of the wealthy requires defending those of the marginalised too. Today, education – encouraging understanding and wisdom rather than knowledge – is a central issue in development because of the profound need to rethink how we view development itself. Once again, art has an incalculable value in communicating these ideas.

If limiting economic growth condemns the poor, especially in the South, and if we really intend to alleviate the stricken earth and its inhabitants, then we must argue for a progressive 'dematerialisation' of growth. We could opt to depend upon biotechnology and genetic engineering, thereby turning the working of all living things on earth, the entire biosphere, to the particular advantage of our own species. Or we can change our habits, a course which presupposes that economic growth and consumption, especially in the North, are not the only end of organised human activity. We have good reason to behave more humbly. The idea that the hierarchy we have spent thousands of years establishing is dangerous to other species and ourselves is new and powerful.

The need to understand the subtleties of the propaganda that shape political and cultural perceptions and which fix the limits of public debate has become more urgent than ever. The 'want over need' ethic is reproduced by a media organisation with transcendent powers of manipulation. Technology and communication may however provide a vehicle for global change. People must be made aware of the long-term consequences of what their consumption patterns are doing to the earth and its inhabitants – only then will we realise a new ethos of equity within and between generations. Attitudes change when the heart responds to what the mind realises; only then can there be a practical call for action. An expansion of information or, more important perhaps, an understanding of the global context, is implied.

International policy makers have not yet come to grips with the full implications of the information revolution. Marginalised groups worldwide – such as the Yanomami in Brazil and Aboriginal groups in Australia – are learning how to use the media and satellite video-conferencing to help link isolated communities, pool information, fight battles over resources or political repression, and access both national and international culture. One can only speculate on how new communication tools and vast quantities of unfamiliar information will be incorporated, translated and adapted cross-culturally. Ideally, there will be a limit to governmental control of digital and fibre-optic transmission, so it might be easier to call political actions to account, to reduce censorship and to mobilise people. An unfettered media and telecommunications revolution could generate a new era of democracy. If governments do intervene, however, a more complete control by vested interests could prevail.

Through the media, we can use cultural means to present a country's society and, simultaneously, to counter racism. The appreciation of the heritage of other cultures is particularly important in race relations for it dispels the false premises upon which ethnocentrism is often based. Art can therefore be a powerful tool for cross-cultural accommodation. Cultural programmes serve a dual function; to foster mutual understanding between countries and to provide background information needed for a better understanding of, and receptivity to, a country's domestic or foreign policy. The information revolution has heightened the importance of both these functions. We need to practice diplomacy at a public level, not just on a governmental one.

Western societies will increasingly have to accommodate other civilisations, whose power will approach that of the West. We see this in several Asian countries – but their values and interests differ significantly. This requires a much more profound understanding of the basic religious and philosophical assumptions of other civilisations, and how they see their interests. It will require identifying those elements of commonality among Western and other civilisations which will help us to coexist. Truth is not absolute. Through other cultures we return with new insights into our own particular society. Art helps demonstrate that we are different, yet one.

It is tempting to speculate that the current interest in the art of the South is partly political, motivated by the shift in global consciousness that has emerged from the new perceptions on ecological problems, the context of the United Nations and the international debt crisis. But there is a fascination with the artifacts which is not paralleled with a respect for the culture of the artist. The repeated emphasis on the failures of the 'developing' world also denies the historical contribution of their artists to 20th century art. And the negative images received of these countries masks the richness, diversity and talent of their cultures.

Knowledge of complex ecological inter-relationships is often expressed in the codified and symbolic forms of myth and ritual as in cave paintings, which probably had specific magical purposes. Similarly, the art of indigenous peoples frequently expresses ecological visions of wholeness and interdependence, drawing on the life forms of their immediate habitat. In the more ecologically balanced state of the Aborigine, the distinction between art and life was meaningless. Living was an art, saturated with the sacramental and the metaphorical. From this we learn that a viable human community does not simply adapt itself to the environment; it builds the environment into its culture and the culture into its environment. It is our cultural and spiritual values which need to form the foundation of community life and stability.

The arts in many parts of Asia, Africa and Latin America are thriving, demonstrating that even in the poorest, often most exploited and environmentally degraded countries, the human spirit prevails. Artists in many parts of the world are aiding the revitalisation of local histories and cultures which can be a resource for building the future, not just a return to the past. This invention, rather than simply a rediscovery of tradition, provides marginalised people with the cultural means to preserve or construct identities without which they cannot survive. These are innovations that must be heeded and encouraged.

The world's cultural diversity is not an accident, it is in part a direct response to global biological diversity. It is the world's cultural diversity, this huge, rich, human resource, that we need to protect and which can provide alternative models of existence. It is important to promote a willingness to accord other societies and indigenous cultures the right to survive in the landscapes and by the means that have sustained them … and could help sustain us. The media and education are necessary to the advancement of cultural pluralism.

To live in hope of a just order brought about by affirmation of one another, is to act creatively in the face of possible destruction. Our unique ability to invent, to conceptualise in language, to create, and above all to influence the future can be employed to approach global problems. Practical possibilities will be found in the recognition that the interests of

North and South, of East and West, of the rich and poor, are ultimately identical. Issues of peace are issues of justice. Peacemaking is not just an idyllic vision – it is policy review and the hard work of breaking patterns of distribution that are ultimately destructive. As a beginning, we should no longer equate the notion of development with wealth production, while recognising how existing economic instruments can provide essential tools for securing equitable progress.

To counter our current failings, we need the better governance of international bodies such as the United Nations. If we can recognise our need of one another and transact peace negotiations which are not based on a spiral of threat or vested interests, we can commit ourselves to the United Nations with some hope. It will not happen unless we ask this of our governments, unless we are all prepared to accept responsibility. The goal of speaking the truth of our failings, and of taking responsibility for them, is to project a better state of affairs corresponding more closely to a set of moral principles – peace, toleration, and the abatement of suffering – into every moment of our political and public life. Following the words of the winner of a Nobel Peace Prize, Aung San Suu Kyi, concepts such as truth, justice and compassion cannot be dismissed as merely idealistic when these are often the only bulwarks which stand against ruthless power.

Focused, determined, enlightened public opinion is the most potent force in the world. It has no equal. It has often been exploited, it has contributed greatly to the common good, and now, more than ever, we need to foster it. It is the possibility of the worst that can make us believe in a new possibility of the best. The reality may lie somewhere in between. Concepts such as goodness, equality and responsibility exist within our languages; moral categories are woven into the fabric of our nature as social, affectionate, language-using beings. An ethical code can, indeed must, be forged out of logic, will and necessity. This belief requires no less than a vision, a vision artists can help realise, a vision humanity must celebrate.

Catherine Thick

August 1995

ANAHI CACERES

In the last decade my artistic work, which includes painting, sculpture and multimedia, has developed parallel to my study in anthropology beginning in the 1980s. The study of a native language brought me even closer to a pre-Colombian culture, and to the old relationship between ceremonial and contemporary art, where an interdisciplinary approach is possible given new philosophical and scientific theories. This gave me a base that is closely bound to the theoretical and ethical concepts underlying *The Right to Hope*. I am now very preoccupied with the search for essential values that celebrate the possibility of evolution and of the transcendence of our culture. As a Latin American, I am conscious of the importance in these times of the profound changes needed in ideals in order to achieve a future that is worthy and just. However, these ideals must be forged in real work; through investigation and the honest contribution of the most spiritual values. *Archaeology of the Third Millennium* is a series of sculptures made up of branches that are pruned, or short naturally, along with hand-made, ecological paper. I raise the idea of the ephemeral nature of our condition, and of the importance of recognising ourselves as an essential and fragile part of a bigger future.

Archaeology of the Third Millennium mixed media with branches and hand-made paper 98x43x39cm

ARGENTINA

Judy Watson and Gonzalo Mella

A Brief History of Colonisation mixed media on canvas 280x800cm

The artists collaborated on this mural in order to rewrite their histories. The brutal invasion of the Americas and Australia has left its legacy with the present generations. Both artists live in Australia and carry their culture within them. Gonzalo is intensely aware of his heritage, and Judy's mother's people are Aboriginal. The work, like a stage drop, re-enacts the resistance against the perpetrators of institutionalised violence, rape and dispossession. As indigenous and marginalised groups are asserting their identity, the rest of the world is beginning to acknowledge their presence and to reassess the past. The words 'Land Rights' are on the back of the mural, an issue which has become prominent in Australia with the recognition of native title over ancestral lands. The appropriation of Aboriginal art is seen by many as a form of symbolic colonisation; simultaneously, Aboriginal groups choose art as a way to express themselves emotionally, morally, socially and culturally, as a way to unite their people.

Australia & Chile

Hamiduzzaman Khan

The sculpture represents harmony between women and nature. If trees live, then humankind will survive. The form, made of wood and metal, symbolises a young mother in the shape of a traditional village hut with some tree saplings. A village hut and tree derive both their structure and vitality from the soil of the country; their sustenance depends on the tender care epitomised by a mother nurturing and looking after a child. There are elements in the sculpture which are rooted in the local culture. The 'tree of life' is a symbol found in the three great religious traditions of this region: Hinduism, Buddhism and Sufistic Islam. The tree is worshipped as a fruit-giver and hence anyone who possesses spiritual power is called 'kalpataru' – a tree which brings forth the desired fruit. The sculpture suggests we need to transcend the local for a global vision. Women of Bengal generally look after the trees in the vicinity of their homesteads; they water them, collect firewood from their fallen branches, use their leaves, fruits, flowers for herbal medicines and in cooking or rituals. Such an intimate relation with trees provides a shining example in a world where increasing commercialisation of the timber trade is depleting forests. Such care gives a ray of hope to a highly mechanised world facing destruction from man's own making. It is therefore necessary to give importance to the values of love and caring and transpose them into the material world, so that we may change the way we look at our environment and give back to the world the right to hope for a better and more harmonious future.

Trees Live then Humankind will Survive wood and bronze 95×53×35cm

Bangladesh

Siron Franco

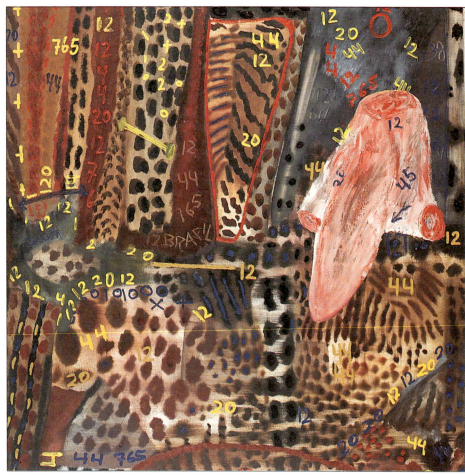

Flesh and Furs oil on canvas 135x155cm

The work of an artist cannot be divorced from his life, or the life of his country. It represents anonymous and distinct realities. This work reveals the impasse of the man who kills to survive. With a man on one side, and an animal on the other, this work depicts life in Brazil, and in South America in general. In a narrower sense, it also depicts the life of a man familiar with poverty, misery and pain, to the extent that he does not try to stop his own suffering or that of others; a needy man whose reality is hunger and lack of esteem. He is a fragile member of a brutalised society where imperialism has never ceased to prevail. In the painting, numbers symbolise anonymity and the predominance of financial values. *Flesh and Furs* depicts the inside (flesh) and outside (fur) of any man or animal. Nameless, ageless, homeless, bound by a common cruel reality, yet expecting from others the right to hope.

Brazil

ANGUS COCKNEY KAANERK

Collaboration marble 38hx43wx15cmd

The Canadian Inuit, my people, traditionally followed the cycle of the seasons. They knew the exact times of the caribou migrations, the return of the waterfowl and the sunbathing of the seals in spring. The hunter knew success depended on being patient and alert. All parts of the animals harvested were used for food, clothing and tools. In a featureless landscape, the Inuit used the snow patterns and the wind for guidance and built *inukshuit* (stone figures) for hunting and directional purposes. These stone figures, which still stand today, resemble people and would direct the migrating caribou toward the waiting hunters. My artistic concept is to combine the spiritual and physical elements of the Inuit culture in order to convey the message that survival means interdependence. These two elements, communicated in the sculpture *Collaboration*, are *inukshuit* and the mythology of Sedna, the sea goddess. The people depend on the marine animals for subsistence and look to Sedna to release them. She is happy when the Inuit shaman has braided her hair. My *inukshuk* has the face of Sedna—her hair is braided, her face is content. The rocks represent the different countries of the world, each separate, but dependent on each other to stand erect. My hope is that all countries will begin to realise the value of collaboration in reaching common goals for the sake of mankind. Only then can we see the face of contentment.

CANADA

Cecilia Martner Peyrelongue

Legend iron, glass, copper, stones 84w×70hcm

My work takes the form of an open book, in iron, which represents the teachings of the past. Inside there are two circles which symbolise the world in the two stages of creation and destruction. Snakes encircle this world symbolising, from pre-Hispanic cultures, wisdom and fertility, and they appear as a spirit of mother earth, constructive and destructive at the same time. The message is that man must change in order to take his rightful place in nature, he must abandon violence as a means of communication and he must respect the laws of nature. I believe that hope of change is based on a profound reflection of the reasons for mankind's past violence, and on the wisdom from those of different epochs and cultures who were in profound contact with nature. We are provoking the wrath of the snake, felt through tremblings and earthquakes, reminding us that man is not all-powerful, but inferior to the power of the earth, in spite of his technological and scientific advances. It also tells us that human beings can live in a world of creation and beauty, through peace and understanding.

Chile & Mexico

Zeng Shanqing and Yang Yanping

Let us bury all violence — war, crime and all destructive acts to the natural environment. We should have the right to hope and we must work to build a peaceful, healthy, as well as beautiful new world for generations to come. The old woman, who is a symbol of the 20th century, comes forth from the shadows of violence and pollution into the radiant light holding before her a newborn, a symbol of the future, towards the sun and green grass. The hands clasping the baby express a prayer of hope for the future, a future without shadows.

Pray for Generations to Come mixed media on rice paper 98x181cm

CHINA

Maria Teresa Cano

Tendido mixed media floor installation 2.5x1.5m

My work shows how inner experiences are in continuous contrast with the outside world, and how cultures are composed of myths and rituals. *Tendido* evokes the kind gesture of setting the table, but the knives also evoke the merciless and violent scenes all too common in a city like Medellin. The family nucleus becomes the place for traditions and for silent thoughts, stored in memory. Each individual participates not only through the senses, but also mentally, expressing his experience and adding it to our common memory. Anecdote thus becomes history as the speaker and the listener communicate at the same time, taking life to art or art to life.

COLOMBIA

Youssouf Bath

This painting is inspired by the unhappy events that have shocked Africa in recent years: famine, war, the destruction of the environment. During war, children, women, old people and the environment are affected the most. After the war, we hope to establish real peace and environmental security, but this is rarely the case. In the right side of the painting we see a child who is a victim of the war; he is wasted away and has a bullet in his chest. The left side shows a woman, the hope of the people. In her stomach – which represents a mystical place like a sacred forest – she is hiding a child, a symbol of rebirth and of liberation of the people. The work, drawn from African culture, myths and beliefs, is very geometric and symbolic: the circles represent everything which is invisible, a union; the triangle, the roof, represents the father, the mother and the children, a trinity; the spiral symbolises elevation, self-sacrifice, the task of effort and spirituality; the vertical lines represent the forest, and the oblique ones represent disorder. The colours are all vegetable dyes – juice from peel and bark, from roots and leaves I have gathered, and chinese ink. Ochre and green represent hope and expectation, red and orange represent flesh, blood and life, and black indicates the forces of the night and the magic of supernatural spirits.

The Disaster; Search for Hope dyes and ink on bark 115x200cm

Cote d'Ivoire

Santiago Rodriguez Olazabal

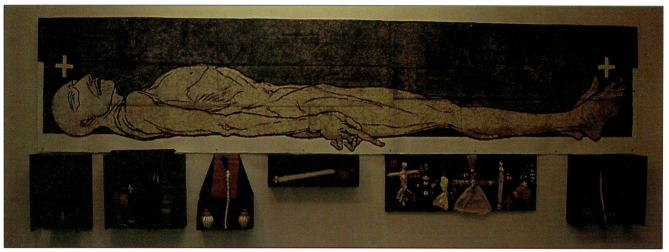

A Dead Man Leaves Behind all his Possessions mixed media on canvas and board 353x119cm

Without spirit, God does not exist. This is a phrase communally spoken in the ceremonies of Cuban *santeria*, a religion of Yoruba ancestry that is very popular in Cuba. My work seeks to create a dialogue with the metaphysical world in which this religion lives, showing the duality between matter and spirit, between the visible and the invisible. This piece of work is inspired by the ceremony of death. Death only constitutes a physical change in the body which allows the spirit to advance towards a superior existence; death is the entrance of human experience to the eternal. The body of the dead man is a store of knowledge which will nourish future generations. His aspiration is that his descendants will recognise the footprints their ancestors have left on the spirit of the land. The dead man's soul shelters hope by which all is transformed.

Cuba

Tony Capellan

Small Hope

One of the most notable functions of art is to reveal new worlds to us. This capacity for communication allows the artist to become a specific medium of expression between the aspirations of the people and the concretisation in images of those aspirations. The desire for justice, sacrifice, love, solidarity, humour and hope can not only be represented through art on the behalf of others but the artworks themselves can influence the audience. In my work, the objects hanging from the children's shirts – such as books, candles or earth – symbolise hope. Hope is setting out to make something, following a path, transcending a limit.

DOMINICAN REPUBLIC

Gazbia Sirry

Hope oil on canvas 150x100cm

My paintings express fantasy and spirituality. The earthly green contrasts the whiteness of the universe and the delicate colours of the people. The human masses, interlocked in each other's arms, try to unite on the edge of the world. They hope for humanity to survive, to unite, and be one.

Egypt

Ivo Lill

There was a discarded glass rock at the bottom of a mountain of glass thrown out from the factory after cleaning the kilns. It was as useless and hopeless as anyone would feel being on the very bottom. I took it and started to work on it, making a pyramid. The pyramid appears to me as a symbol of aspiration, moving from the large base toward a brilliant top which can be achieved after the hard work of a lifetime, after clearing up your desires and eliminating all that is unnecessary. The rings in the pyramid are similar to those which remain on the surface after throwing a stone into water; meaning that on the way up there is always the possibility of falling into the depths. They symbolise all the difficulties and feelings of hopelessness and desperation. The problem is how to fight them, which comes through work and belief. And the higher you go, the purer the pyramid is, the more exactly and clearly you can see your goal. The top of the pyramid is turning: it is quite common that you discover when almost reaching the top, that all your life you have moved in the wrong direction. But staying at the bottom would never reveal this. Only on this very high level are you able to realise that there is no straight way to the top. Looking deep into yourself and having all the experience and knowledge you mastered on the way up, you are able to choose a new and more perfect goal. Everyone has the right to hope wherever they come from – even starting from the bottom of the mountain – and nothing can be achieved without hard work and difficulties, or without hope and belief in yourself.

Aspiration glass

ESTONIA

ZERIHUN YETMGETA

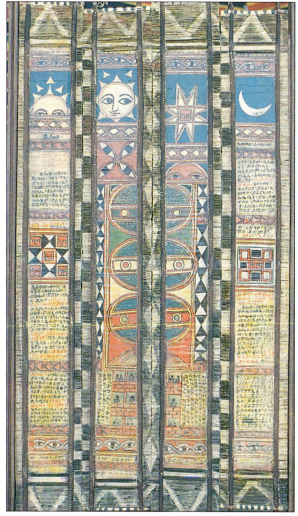

Magic Art mixed media on bamboo 105x54cm

My work, *Magic Art*, is painted in acrylic colour on woven bamboo strips covered in goatskin. The method of painting, the use of colour and flatness, draws on the tradition of Ethiopian church painting. I transform my experiences, the things I see and hear, and what I feel about the world. The symbols are from the magic scroll, a medicine for the eye of the devil, and draw on the written language, Giz, one of Ethiopia's early languages. The magic scroll still exists in some parts of the continent but it is largely forgotten, so I am trying to revive it, bringing it back to life with passion to help rid the world of evil.

ETHIOPIA

OSMO RAUHALA

As all living creatures on earth, human beings depend on the information received from our surroundings in order to survive as a species. Religion, art and philosophy are ways for us to understand the world around us. Our present information system is said to be the most efficient in the history of mankind. Space technology and theoretical physics have opened up the possibility of creating a new narrative describing the structure of the universe and nature. The mass media have made knowledge a consumer commodity, compressed into a mean value, and the information which remains outside this is meaningless. It is this 'unsaid information' which interests me. In the past, knowledge was connected to the capacity of the human mind to perceive and understand information consciously or subconsciously. *Cosmic Memory* is about this information, common to all human beings in spite of their cultural backgrounds, which is transmitted through dreams, feelings, instincts, and by other ways known and still unknown, enabling all living creatures to be in touch with each other. It is about what the spirit perceives and trusts.

Cosmic Memory monotype 91.4x63.5cm

FINLAND

Owusu Ankomah

Sympathy acrylic on canvas 200x240cm

In everyone lies a humanitarian essence which enables us to deepen our interest in human relationships. Hence my interest in the human psyche and its perpetual development and my fascination for the strong, harmoniously built physique which symbolises the beauty of the human race. This concept of perfection based on sympathy and power inspires me to create works of art which deal with the ambiguity of neo-fascism, and with the readiness of the strong to help and protect the weak. This is a trait which lies in the traditions of most of the peoples of Africa. I respect cultural traditions from all over the world, especially the pre-colonial art heritage of Africa which plays an important part in my work; without learning from the past, we cannot made a conscious effort in the present to hope for a better future.

GERMANY & GHANA

El Anatsui

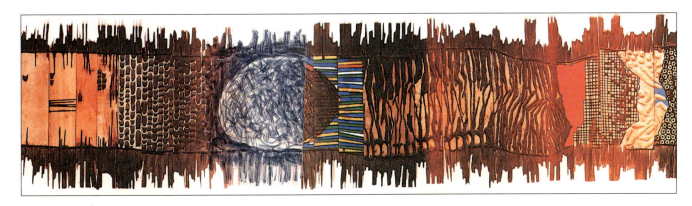

Unfolding the Scroll of History wood and tempera 60x629cm

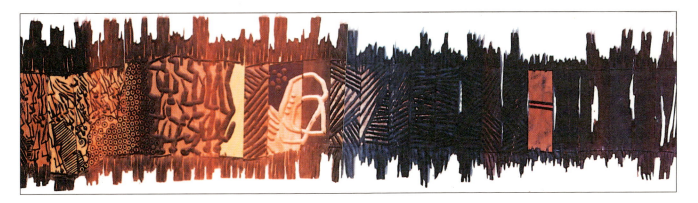

The idea of a scroll made up of a variety of wood, different in colours, textures and grain, suggests not only cooperation and unity, but also continuity and cyclicity of experience and events. History – as hinted at by the pictograms, signs and symbols derived mostly from my region of the world – has continued to reveal to mankind that kind events, or even places and things, are not static entities; they are in constant motion and change. Hope resides in our knowledge that events come and go, even repeat themselves, but mankind survives and grows by the experience, as the script of our collective scroll unfolds, revealing new texts or recalling familiar ones in time and place.

GHANA & NIGERIA

EFRAIN RECINOS

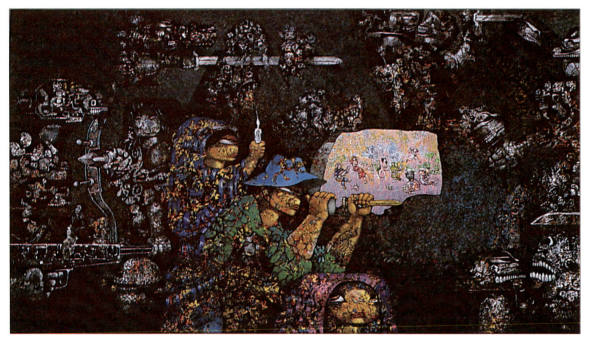

Construction of the Future oil on durapanel 1×2m

I believe that if we all make our best effort to free ourselves from the awful conditions that persist everywhere in the world, it will be possible for our civilisation to find a more humane way of living together. In the painting, a sculptor is making an opening in a dark wall riddled with violence. The opening is a window to the world we are all hoping for. The painting is full of contrasts, depicting the world of destruction and the world of peace. The world of peace is small as yet but will lighten the darkness due to the intensity of the love within it. I believe that an artist has, through his work, the right to hope to free himself and help those who feel as he does, from the world of destruction which persists around us and to live together more humanely in a world of love.

GUATEMALA

Marilene Phipps

The *Prayer House* which stands in the Haitian countryside is a Houmfort (voodoo temple). The Virgin represents Mother Earth, with the desolate landscape expressing the depth of her suffering. The saints which come to her rescue are symbols of both the spiritual realm and of the active power of the physical realm. Their monumental size in relation to the building attests to the importance of spirituality for Haitians. The earth's distress is being heard. The roof casts a shadow; the shadow is not dense, the sun comes through in strips of light, there is hope. The shadow serves as a stage for prayer, work and celebration. Haitian voodoo is in itself a testimony to the sophistication of minds which adapted African gods to the Christian pantheon. The humble appearance of the house is misleading: while it does relate to present economic difficulties, it also shows how the imagination can come to the rescue when life is hard. As we try to create a better world for our children, let us not permit arrogance, bigotry and selfishness to carry the day. May all the prayer houses of the world be the people's legacies of the right to hope.

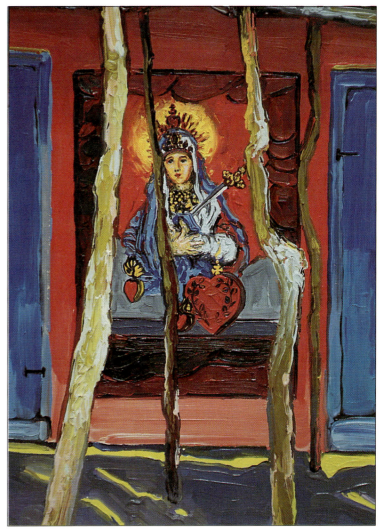

Prayer House (detail) oil on canvas 36"x48"

Haiti & USA

VIVAN SUNDARAM

Gun Carriage installation

Gun Carriage is a sculpture about death, of a man caught in the cross-fire of religious fundamentalism. The man is also the victim of oppression of the majority against the minority. Images of death in our time are imploded into our lives. We are made to become passive viewers to these moving images. By using a newspaper photograph of a dead man in the middle of the street against a large dump, I want to insist on the recall of a tragic moment. Because of the way I have cropped and pasted the photograph on a curved surface, the man looks as if he is embalmed. The fragile photograph is protected by a thick plastic sheet, a bullet-proof screen, a possible memorial for the victim. The memorial object is placed on a large rusted steel trolley, a mobile pedestal. This death is not for burial, the emblematic image will not pass into another life. This death will be carried ceremoniously on a gun carriage, and pulled through the streets of life. By bringing various elements together to become sculpture, the viewer is given the task of handling a disturbing image in a minimalist form. A tragedy offers itself for reflection – if not for action, action based upon hope.

INDIA

Ansupati

Tribute to Bosnia-Herzegovina wood

I created *Tribute to Bosnia-Herzegovina* in 1992. The work has the form of an instrument of a traditional game once popular among Javanese children, called *dakon*. By using the shape of the instrument, I wish to remind people of the children who always suffer most in war, and whose horror remains with them for the rest of their lives. The form also resembles a boat which is an important symbol of the afterlife journey in the indigenous beliefs of the peoples in the Pacific region. Originally, round holes were carved on the *dakon*, where seeds, pebbles or sea shells were placed. I carved four holes of significant shapes. Each of the holes has a lid, making the whole piece like a puzzle. The shapes are a star, as a symbol of religion or military force; a key hole, representing the conscience; a heart, representing love; and a cross, representing humanity as well as religion. The juxtaposition of these different shapes presents us with several possibilities; the suffering of others and our future should not be treated as a game as if we are unaware of the consequences of our choices.

INDONESIA

Gizella Varga Sinai

Forgotten Paradise (detail) oil on canvas 120x80cm

The remains of a wall, worn out by time, war and natural disasters stands before a land once inhabited by people. On the wall is a faded fresco of the Garden of Eden, a beautiful paradise where human beings have always longed to live, the place where no evil exists, where nature glows in her abundance, where souls are at peace. A small girl is anxiously watching from behind the wall. She has seen the faded paradise on the wall and she hopes that someday she might find herself in that free and peaceful land.

Iran & Hungary

Kimio Tsuchiya

Moon   wood   375cmwx100cmd

A Celtic myth asserts that once, long ago, every form of earthly life shared a common language. But an angry god took this language away from human beings as a punishment for their argumentativeness, their jealousy and their pettiness. From then on, human beings lacked the ability to communicate, not only with other forms of life, but also with each other. The dire consequences of this have become manifest in the history of this troubled, violent century. How to return to this ancient state? Can we create a vision that encompasses all cultures? A vision that transcends race and religion, boundaries and borders, geography and ideology; a vision which ensures that the future will be a time of peace and plenty, of hope and happiness. The time has come. The moon has risen. But can we do it before the moon fades into the dawn?

Japan

KHALID KHREIS

Change acrylic on wood

The idea of my artwork was inspired by the title of *The Right to Hope* project. I have tried to emphasise the meaning of change, the fundamental change from our present existence toward a better one. The educational aspect of the exhibition made me think of creating an ever changing artwork; any of the small-sized squares could be fitted within the large square, each time forming a whole new image. This gives the viewer an opportunity to participate in the creation process by altering the squares, which I tried to unify in colour, according to their own concepts and views. I chose the white colour for the small square at the centre of the large one as a symbol of global peace, hope and brotherhood among nations. Blue stands for a universal outlook; ochre symbolises the sun, clarity and justice; and, finally, burnt sienna for our mother earth, a symbol of fertility and eternity. This work is part of a step towards fostering a unified world, and toward eliminating the artificial boundaries and obstacles standing in the way of its realisation.

JORDAN

Steve Ngige

Portrait of Love wood 51hx66wx41cmd

Hope refers to the future and the future depends on young people the world over. Our children depend on the present adult generation under whose care they are charged. My madonna is a portrait of love, with the mother as a symbol of humanity, of the present generation, of all people of the world. The child is symbolic of the youth without whom we have no future. More often than not, the young have no direct role in the moulding of their destiny. Tomorrow has the right to influence today as yesterday influenced today; it is thus upon humanity to invest its love in today's youth for the sake of generations to come. To love them means dedicating all efforts toward a better future, to the children whose right it is to hope.

Kenya

Duck–Hyun Cho

I have prepared an installation using boxes for this exhibition. The origin of these boxes varies; US military cartridge cases, antiques, and even some very new ones. Some are closed, some are left open. The open boxes differ in their contents; some contain drawings and blank canvas, others are empty. The images, graphite and charcoal on canvas, are from old Korean, Japanese and American portraits. I have put lifelike drawings of newly-born babies in the boxes which have a built-in light to bring out the brightness and warmth of the baby's face. The boxes are womb-like. Babies are born from their mothers womb, out of the box of birth. Then they grow up in the invisible box of this world. As they grow up into their adulthood, they make many different invisible boxes around them. And finally they return to another box, the coffin, when they die. Mankind's intelligence has influenced the development of society. Even though we have little control over birth and death, civilisation is dependent on our capabilities. My boxes are the containers of this truth.

Light of Hope Installation

KOREA

Ariffin Mohd Ismail

Meeting Point bronze

My creative work is currently focused on our environment. I am looking at the political implication of the decades of events that are causing a major ecological crisis. Global stability and relationships amongst countries of the world are threatened. These international concerns need to be shared in order for us to solve the problems in the interest of us all. It requires commitment, time and money. There is an unfortunate tendency toward overcoming the crisis by manipulating the present world's political and economic structure. Economically, any continuous effort to restructure the global society has to be done based on its socio-economic needs without imposing the interests of any world power. Such a destructive situation faces the world today and the need to highlight it at the top of the world's agenda has become part of my responsibility. I take advantage of being an artist; I express my belief that our collective values should be shared; we need to stand as one voice of obligation for the sake of one another and the earth. My work expresses the need for compromise between all of us. The spirit of humanity, as a single nation, should reach out regardless of divisions between 'North' and 'South'.

Malaysia

GROUPE BOGOLAN KASOBANE

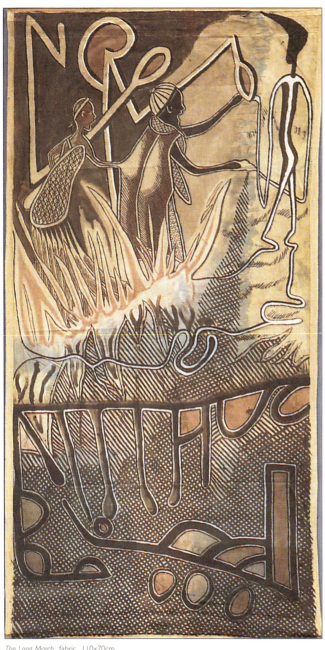

The Long March fabric 110x70cm

A walk towards life, a walk towards the discovery of others, towards the exchange of friendships, a walk towards the good of being individuals and a collective. Such is the message of my artwork which gives homage to all those who fight for a better world. The motif is a scene of characters who follow one another. They are received with open arms in the midst of luminous rays symbolising the earth, tolerance and solidarity. The long march, that of man in search of his equilibrium, is presented through a metaphor in which the heron, a migratory, is a hero; the bird's arrival in the Sahel desert is always considered an exceptional event. The heron foretells rain and of a love rendezvous between the flora and fauna. The bird invites us all to admire the abundance of nature, a joy which we must preserve at all cost; it is necessary for our survival. My message is a call for everyone facing the problems of the world to walk towards one another for the future of our mother earth.

MALI

Victor Anicet

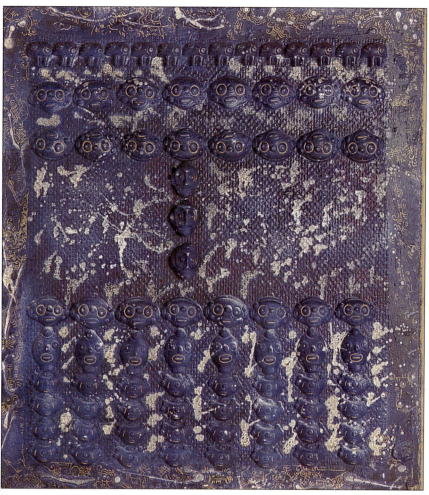

Tray mixed media 150x97cm

The tray is made of wood and is strong enough to carry stones to build houses, wide enough to be carried on the head of the black slave; it is also used for washerwomen's laundry and for merchants' wares. It travels through space and time in the Caribbean, like a boat that the American Indians sailed in from island to island. The tray carries *adornos* – pieces of Amerindian pottery which resemble masks, and this constitutes the framework of the piece. Each *adorno* is a zémi, a god, a symbol. The tray sails like a boat with us and all our hopes as passengers, towards our future, towards modernity, towards progress.

Martinique

Nestor Quinones

Tree of Life wood, cord, wire 3.4lx3wx0.8dm

For this exhibition, I worked with a group, maintaining no one particular aesthetic stance. This enabled us to embrace a collective consciousness and made us realise that difficulties between individuals will not stop arising. Therefore it is vital, for the regeneration of the future, to assimilate these differences and remain yet remain committed to one another. The *Arbol de la Vida* (Tree of Life) is a traditional form of Mexican art. Primarily, it symbolises the basic source of life. This is the conception with which we, as a community, made the tree. Root, trunk, branch, flower, fruit and seed, reflect the value we place in our group relationship. The seed is a product equivalent to our collective conscience. Our respect for the vital part —the root — gave us the opportunity to live and work in a common trunk in organic diversity, maintaining equilibrium and respecting individuality. All human beings share the earth as a unique source of life and we need to renew our consciousness in order to restructure our values and goals for this future in which we are already living. The Arbol de la Vida has two faces, one shows the side of man's self-destructive power, dry and destructive in its root, the other shows union and hope.

MEXICO

Joe Madisia

This work is dedicated to peace. It is a plea for unity among human beings, plants, and animals. The design is centred on a tree whose roots change into hands gripping onto one another, and eyes looking at one another, symbolising the interdependence of all life. On top of the soil, fumes emerge from clay pots which pass through the leaves and fruit to the sky, symbolizing the influence the earth's nutrients have on all those walking, living and depending on its bounty. The top of the stem of the tree changes into a hand holding the sky in which fly three white birds of peace. In the background, a woven printed texture shows the interdependence of nations and communities. In short, this work symbolises unity, and shows that the tree can only produce good fruit if its roots have unity with other trees in a rich soil. As each tree has many roots and branches, we can state Unity in Diversity and Diversity in Unity. The trees stand together in solidarity, contributing to each other's well-being.

Tree of Unity Print 1.1x1.4m

NAMIBIA

Nike Olaniyi Davies

The Tree of Life indigo batik 213×122cm

This piece is an expression of the traditions of different peoples throughout the world. I chose the tree in the centre to represent the world, as it is strong and has many branches and leaves of which no two are the same, representing the different countries. Beside the tree, are the people of the world who all struggle, laugh and hope for a better life. In life, we take from the Earth and so must give something back without causing waste. I see a lot of art in life; my art has helped me realise most of my hopes and wishes. When I did this work, I thought about all the troubles in the world, especially here in Africa. I show symbols of what is taking place in my world as I see it through art. The batik reflects my west African environment with its dust, its heat and smells, its movements and sounds, its legends, dreams and patterns. The sun is the brightest of all my symbols and is everyone's hope for a better, united life.

Nigeria

Laila Shawa

Children of War, Children of Peace silkscreen on canvas 2 panels, 230x90cm

My work depicts children in war zones, and although it is based on the children of Gaza, they could be from any war zone in the world. Children are the future of this world; if they are scarred, they will be unbalanced and will resort to violence to resolve even the simplest of conflicts. They would feel, even during peace, that to lay down their arms would endanger their existence. The panels differ only in the background colour; in *The Time of Peace*, the state of war is not altered except cosmetically, and this will remain as long as the roots of conflict are not addressed. The boy does not put down his weapon, but simply shifts his posture, becoming even more menacing. The traumatisation of children through exposure to violence must be addressed universally if we are to dare to hope for a future on this earth.

Palestine & UK

Monica Gonzalez and Osvaldo Salerno

Wash and Wear linen cloth, serigraphy, tin plate

The piece is composed of diverse elements; mainly bed sheets and metal buckets. The structure has complex meanings related to the human condition. On one side, there are highly dramatic connotations: the representation of the man is upside down, implying a marked alteration of his natural position, and suggesting an outrage against his dignity. The impression of the human body reminds us of Christ's shroud, of the image of Leonardo da Vinci, and of the vestiges that a sleeping body leaves in his vigil or dreams. On the other hand, the piled buckets on the floor refer to the woman's domestic world, opposed to the violence of the image. Objects of daily use appear visually supporting the projection of a fantastic, misshaped world. The buckets are custodians of a certain hope: they contain supplementary bed sheets. These are linen cloths of ephemeral whiteness that patiently expect to drain away the signs of pain, of human guilt and misconduct; they express an effort has been made once again with conviction, enthusiasm and hope.

Movimiento Manuela Ramos

Restaurant and Market arpilleria (fabric applique) 40x52cm

My work represents purchases from the market and the preparation of food, and is inspired by the community strategies used by poor women to organise themselves collectively to confront the problem of hunger in their families — especially among children — and their communities. They are trying to protect themselves against the deterioration of their quality of life and the deepening economic crisis. The growing presence of these groups implies the need for change in the relationships of power and in the condition of women. Over time, these organisations have consolidated and strengthened themselves. They provide a democratic discussion forum for the women who negotiate with public and private companies, demonstrating their leadership capabilities. On a personal level they promote discipline and respect for others, recognising the valuable contribution made by individuals in ensuring a better future.

PERU

LOUISE METZGER

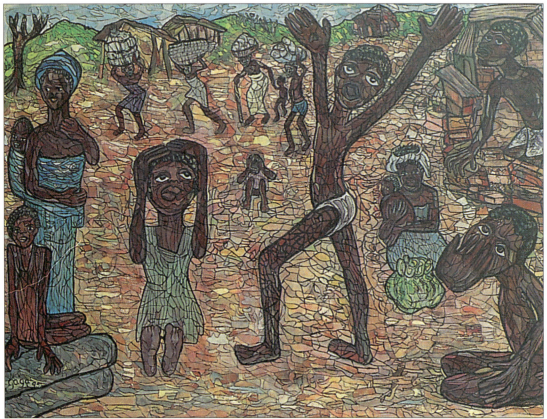

Hope oil on canvas 93x64cm

Today we live in a world seemingly devoid of love or sympathy for others. In almost every part of the world we see manifestations of man's inhumanity to man, resulting in the displacement and homelessness of millions of human beings. The hands and minds of the human race have changed the planet by destroying the surface of the earth, nature, wildlife and even mankind. The whole world is in turmoil and seemingly without hope; there is clearly a need to foster and protect understanding, friendship and solidarity. Children are the leaders of tomorrow and must be nurtured for their important role. We must therefore concentrate our efforts on our young ones for they more than anyone else have the right to hope for a better world, a world worth living for.

SIERRA LEONE

Marko Pogacnik

Cosmogramme carved stone

My art work is usually not bound to the gallery structure. Mainly I work within the ambience of those landscapes which have been in one way or another disturbed by human misuse. To meet such conditions, I have developed several methods of ecological healing which are similar to acupuncture of the human body. I position stone pillars on sensitive points, a method I call *lithopuncture*, to bring about healing of the earth. The lithopuncture stones could not serve properly without specific patterns carved on their surface, which I call *cosmogrammes*. For this exhibition, I chose a three-headed mountain in the Julian Alps named Triglav, in Lokvice, Slovenia. This mountain is a symbol for the essence of Slovenia and represents the main feature of its coat of arms. I designed a specific cosmogramme representing a transformation of the coat of arms and carved it on a stone slab, serving as a portable lithopuncture stone for the exhibition, carrying with it the quality of the mountain in Lokvice. Stand in silence and feel its power of healing.

SLOVENIA

WILLEM BOSHOFF

Bottled Hope glass, seeds

'Bottled Hope' is an artwork of seeds, especially made for *The Right to Hope* project. Seeds tell of untapped creative forces, of hope. Seeds are the words we sow. In South Africa, the seeds of negotiation are sprouting into understanding and change. Often, seed is expected to perform above itself, to grow in the most infertile and hostile places. Magical seeds can grow in rocks, thistles and concrete. In another work, I revived the seeds of dead words by asking blind people to make them grow in an art gallery, a place where the blind are least expected. South Africa has a divergent population of multifarious indigenous and international persuasions so shattered that only a special alchemist can unite them. 'Bottled Hope' is a mixed bag of South African seeds. Some, like the robust acacia, were painstakingly collected from the wild. Weeds and flower seeds were sampled from exotic plants in gardens, and miniscule mustard seeds (that grow so large) were rescued from being eaten. I bottled seeds that nourish and heal into 256 medicine bottles, to form a kind of social patchwork. A layer of fertile earth at the bottom of each bottle supports an evolutive pyramid under a sheltering sky, all made of seed.

SOUTH AFRICA

Rashid Diab

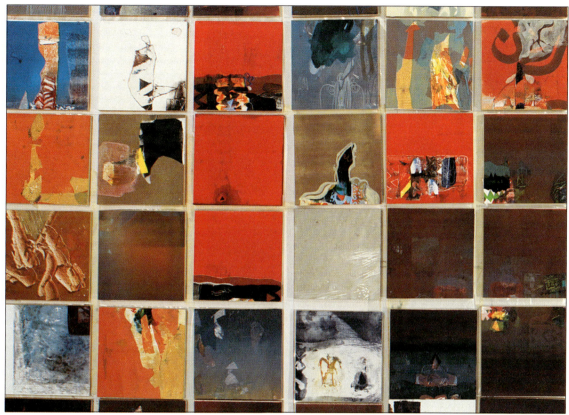

Diary of an Immigrant (detail) mixed media 25x25cm panels

My work reflects a synthesis of my Sudanese heritage and an awareness of contemporary artistic development in Europe. The imagery and symbols range from Arabic illuminations and calligraphic designs, animals, human figures, traditional folk and historical motifs, to mythical and mask-like African motifs. Through my art, I am most concerned about universality, that art is ultimately the connection between human beings, and sustains the cultures which finally indicate the material part of civilisation. We, as human beings, are the bearers of this task. This is my creed and I wish to communicate it. Thus, it is not a mere coincidence of other times or an incarnation of some moment; it is more than that, it is actually a reflection of the human being as a conclusion, a material result of the species which I tried to express in this work. The colour and form illustrate moments of sorrow, happiness, despair and hope, but the most important element is that of nostalgia for this universal world.

Sudan & Spain

JOHAN MHLANGA

Two People and a Fish wood

Once, a long time ago, when men still had horns, there were plenty of fish in the rivers, but today fish are not so plentiful. When people go to fish, they normally throw the fish over their backs and it hangs there, lifeless. In my carving I have placed the fish stretching up to the heaven, still breathing. This symbolises the life energy of nature, that the fish will survive and will bring life to man in turn. I believe that God took away our horns because there was too much fighting. I am angry at those who do not work, who do not see what they can do with their own hands. If we could live together in peace as God intended, there would be no fighting over land, we would work to provide for our families and there would be life in the rivers and harmony on earth.

SWAZILAND

Gongkar Gyatso

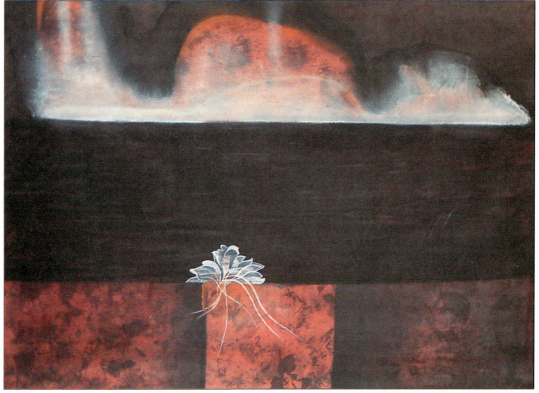

Lotus oil on canvas

I painted this work in 1991. Listening to the BBC and hearing of the violence and bloodshed in this world, images of the 1989 Tiananmen Square massacre and the many uprisings in Lahasa city, filled my mind. The black horizontal strip cutting the painting represents an ocean of ignorance and suffering that every human being has been immersed in from the beginning of time. This ocean is placid, representing people's blindness to the realities of the human condition and their acquiescence to their own enslavement. In the horizon behind we can see immense eruptions of fire and lava which represent human conflict especially in its ultimate form of nuclear warfare. It also stands for the tremendous power of natural disasters like fires, volcanoes and earthquakes which signal man's increasing destruction of his own environment. The white lotus floating peacefully on the ocean of suffering, unaffected by war and violence represents the Buddha potential within all of us to eventually overcome negative forces and gain true understanding of ourselves and our condition. The symbol of the lotus is taken from Tibetan *thangka* painting and represents the purity of the human spirit which though sunk in the pain and ignorance of the wheel of existence, will eventually grow out into the clear air and pure light to liberation.

Tibet

HANDAN BORUTECENE

Cosmic Envelopes (detail)   lead plate and bay leaves

I cannot comprehend the seductive effects of power which so frequently result in war. We are experiencing the most important changes in a painful way. Money is now a more influential social dynamic than ideology. The market system, acting as the eye and ear of the ruler, forms the individual into any shape it likes. This structure causes some people to be timid, some become fundamentalists, even killers. Worst of all, we are alienating the truth. Perhaps the memory of earth, of its people can help us find a solution. I use the symbol of one of the oldest communication models, the envelope, a symbol for one-to-one communication. They are hung in a Pythagorean order, reflecting fire, air, water and earth. Civilizations, from the ancient to the modern, are recorded in part through layers and layers of communications. Recalling these 'conversations' helps develop an understanding between individuals, between people and nature, they stand for peace among the traditions of the planet we live on. Bay has been used since ancient times, it figures frequently in mythology, it is a symbol for peace. I have put bay leaves for each state on earth in the lead envelopes. I put dead bay leaves on the ground to symbolize past civilizations. We need peace between civilizations because there is no ultimate victor through violence. We need true relations between individuals, and between people and nature, more than ever. Through my artwork, I use my right to hope.

TURKEY

ALEXANDER BORODIE

Joining the Past and the Present enamel

My work is based on the unity of opposites. New colours are applied layer upon layer on the canvas of our life. But nothing disappears without trace. The present coats the past, but they are both inseparably linked. One serves as a base for the other and cannot be removed. The work focuses on the link between different times, especially in ancient Ukraine where masterpieces have been systematically destroyed for centuries. A thousand years ago, paganism and Christianity merged and gave birth to a renewed culture. In my work I try to join the past and the present, to revive forgotten but still relevant images and symbols. In this work, the final one of a series, cross-sections of time are presented. There is a plant ornament, the silhouette of a crucifix, part of a stone Scythian image, a character from a poem by Shevchenko, as well as elements of the modern age. The golden background symbolises the vast wheat fields of the Ukraine. Background coats of different materials and melted enamel represent the multilayered structure of nations. Fusing these organic materials, fire thus repeats the birth of the Earth. This perception of depth and colour through time by means of art gives us the right to hope for continued renewal.

UKRAINE

One World Quilt Group

One World Quilt 4x7m

This is the story of cooperation, sharing, networking and commitment to change. It is about making our world a better place for all who live in it. The quilt is a testimony to our common future, a focus for ongoing exploration and joint education concerning the issues which we hope will make our world more just and fair. To publicise and focus on issues raised at the 1992 United Nations Earth Summit, the Group decided to invite many community groups from the area to contribute towards a large community quilt. The project was a resounding success and it was realised that women and children were waiting to find an appropriate form of expression to voice their needs and concerns. The quilt has been exhibited widely and has inspired others to be created; it is part of a growing worldwide movement. While working together, the women and children discuss and think about some of the issues we face, such as racial conflict, women's struggles, conservation of nature, the protection and education of the world's children. The quilt is a celebration of life and an expression of the responsibility we all share in contributing to change in our world.

United Kingdom

Rimer Cardillo

Lost Forest Reliquaries wood, copper, embossed paper, plexiglass 43hx28wx36cml (closed)

This work is part of a series entitled *Lost Forest Reliquaries*. These containers come from ancient Judeo-Christian traditions where sacred items were preserved and venerated. Sometimes these altars were portable and used during a people's exodus. My box shrines contain autobiographical or cultural narratives expressed by small pieces of trees, branches from very old forests, seeds, stones and found objects. In this box I include a broken branch from a remote tree found on the shores of the Hudson river. Aged by the elements, its present state is as powerful as its living past. The disappearance of native peoples and their natural environment in our present world is the constant source of these works of art, aiming towards a hopeful communication between the past and the present.

Uruguay & USA

Ricardo Benaim

Homage to the Three Kingdoms mixed media 130x200cm

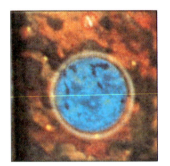

My work addresses the ecological dimension of *The Right to Hope*; I am attempting to balance the relationship between humans and nature. I understand ecology as a way of relating living beings and a balance of habitats. In my painting, I present a particular vision mixing fate, science, fractals, the natural and the emotive response to the interrelationship of the three existing kingdom – animal, vegetable and mineral. It is a homage to nature itself, breaking down its own essence and articulating a simple language formed by tiny fragments placed in order, offering an integral, didactic and sensitive reading. In this piece, we can appreciate bird feathers, squid skin, minerals, stones, leaves and roots. A digital impression of rocky transformations and seeds. All of this is placed on an industrial canvas which has served as the protective floor of my studio, transporting a series of experiences and situations, synthesising them onto a physical space representing the three kingdoms of nature.

Venezuela

BUU CHI

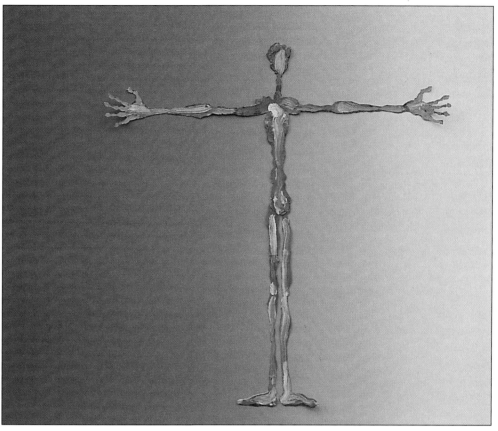

Requiem oil on paper 76x58cm

I use my paintings to express my thoughts and feelings about the sad and dark side of life. Painting is an international language, in which all people of the world can communicate and share. This for me is a sublime happiness. *Requiem* is my way of praying to the dead, also my way of causing human beings to reflect on the preciousness of life. People cannot live without humanity. And only with humanity can people hope...

VIETNAM

GLADMAN ZINYEKA

Homage to Refugees carved stone

In my sculpture, I have tried to highlight the plight of refugees universally. It is my intention that this sculpture, through my inner spirit, portrays the catastrophe represented by refugees of the world. The plight of the parent and child is a heart-breaking story in today's world. We are fortunate to have people and organisations who are doing their best to try and solve their problems. As we are now going into the 21st century, is it not time that mankind and the powers who control the lives of nations look deeper into the root causes which bring about such suffering? Is it not true that the world is our country and mankind our brethren? I believe these questions can somehow be heard through all mediums of expression. Any form of art, music or philosophy, could be applied to the `poverty' of this world. Let us unite and all work towards easing this pain.

ZIMBABWE

1

Nothing Short of a Miracle

Archbishop Desmond Tutu

Let us not forget just what the situation was like here in South Africa and where we come from. We are experiencing the victory of justice over oppression, of democracy over totalitarianism; the unjust and immoral laws of apartheid have been broken. A veritable miracle is unfolding before our very eyes.

We must remember the past, but not be imprisoned by it. Whereas resources were invested to demean one another, now we want to invest our resources in developing an equitable future for all. It *can* happen, good can prevail over evil. So South Africa, quite unexpectedly, has become a beacon of hope for the world.

The international community has a huge share in this victory. You watched, and prayed, and celebrated with us. You were marvellous in supporting the imposition of the sports boycott and financial, as well as other, sanctions. It was this pressure, more than anything else, which ensured that Namibia is independent today and that Nelson Mandela walked to freedom. And the international community is willing us to succeed; especially now, at a time when we are all somewhat disillusioned by the sad tales emanating from many parts of Africa.

Perhaps what is most remarkable is the almost universal lack of bitterness among those who have suffered. God appears to have given Africans a remarkable capacity to forgive. We have seen it happen in Kenya after the Mau Mau uprising when predictions were made that Kenya would become the white man's grave. It turned out differently under President Kenyatta, the erstwhile devil incarnate! It is happening similarly in Zimbabwe; President Mugabe surprised his detractors after his election victory when he spoke about reconciliation, reconstruction, rehabilitation, and not revenge. Anger and hatred are the things that gnaw at us; they are corrosive and destructive of the harmony that is indispensable for building a community.

Africans have a thing called *umbuntu*; it is about the essence of being human, it is part of the gift that Africa is going to give to the world. It embraces hospitality, caring about others, being willing to go that extra mile for the sake of another. We believe that a person is a person through other persons; that my humanity is caught up, bound up, inextricably in yours. When I dehumanise you, I inexorably dehumanise myself. The solitary human being is a contradiction in terms, and therefore you seek to work for the common good because your humanity comes into its own in community, in belonging.

We are made for interdependence. The law of our being is the law of complementarity. I don't have everything that would make me self-sufficient, and God did that deliberately, so that I should know my need of you. You have gifts that I don't have and I have gifts that you don't have; then I need you and you need me for us to be completed. Even the wealthiest and most powerful countries know they cannot exist on their own. They can have a fullness only in relationship to other countries; so there is something in the make-up of the world that forces us to realise that we are done for if we think we can exist on our own.

There is a link too between human beings and the rest of nature. It is important for us to care about the soil

because the soil is not just a thing. When we treat it with contempt, it has a way of backfiring on us; it is not just because the soil is then denuded, but it seems to actually do something to us because in a real sense the earth *is* our mother. And God has been generous in the diversity that happens in all of his creations – animal and plant forms, human beings, cultural practices – and we are actually at our best when we give play to that diversity.

What is it about creation that moves the soul? Many people whose spiritual commitments are not with conventional religion or institutions report their encounters with nature in expressly spiritual terms. We need to develop a sense of wonder and reverence for the earth and for one another. I believe spirituality cannot be separated from social action. Prayer leads me deeper into the struggle for justice in the world. And our struggle for justice drives me deeper into prayer. The struggle for peace, equality and environmental security is one with and not separate from the spiritual life. I do not distinguish between hope and belief.

Our imagination and creativity are also linked to transcendence. As can be seen in art, even back as far as the cave paintings, there is an interconnection in the things of the spirit, in the things that seek to represent the spirit. Many societies see the artist as one who mimics divine reality and, in so doing, becomes a link between the invisible spiritual world and the tangible world of flesh and bone. The role of art and culture – in its highest and most common forms – is to reveal God, divinity, among us.

God put us in a wonderful universe, but we have to make our way often in situations of great ambiguity where it is never a matter simply of this is right, that is wrong. Many are scared of the exhilarating business of trying to work out what is right. I am full of hope for the future of South Africa because we are an extraordinary country with quite remarkable people. Yes, we are plagued by violence, much of it politically motivated, much of it grounded in poverty. We deplore it – even a single death is one too many. We do our bit in the church to defuse tensions and to act as agents for reconciliation and peace. But it is quite amazing that the violence is mostly non-racial, given all that blacks have suffered at the hands of white oppressors, and that so far no one has sought to embark on an orgy of slaying whites. Nor is the violence even ethnic, despite the obnoxious label given to it by the media of black-on-black violence; I have never heard them describe Bosnia or Northern Ireland as the scenes of white-on-white violence. Perhaps we in South Africa can show the world that freedom depends on the freedom that *others* enjoy.

We are the rainbow people of God. We are still having to try to work out what it means to celebrate our diversity. That is not easy, because people have tended to denigrate what was different and use this as a reason to persecute and exploit one another. There is a basic selfishness in almost all of us, so we have to keep struggling against it for goodness to emerge triumphant. And let's not be cynical, for there is a great deal of good in the world which ultimately overcomes the evil.

Never doubt that a small group of committed people can change the world. In fact, that is about all that ever has, so just imagine the potential if we were *all* to join hands. The Indian philosopher Modamyetz taught us, 'Be not a whisper that is lost in the wind; be a voice that is heard above the storms of life.' For God operates in each and every one of us. It is in the power of everybody, with a little courage, to hold out a hand to someone different, to listen, to attempt to increase the quantity of kindness and humanity in the world.

I believe God has called South Africa to a special vocation. I am hopeful because God wants South Africa to succeed for one simple reason; when we get it right, we will provide the world with a paradigm of how to solve its problems. For South Africa has most of the world's problems writ small: black versus white, poverty versus affluence, industrialised and sophisticated versus developing and simple, large majority versus various minorities, pluralism and diversity. We are learning that it is essential to see events in the world from the perspective of the outcast, the

maltreated, the powerless – in short, from the perspective of those who suffer. We will then know the truth and the truth will help set us free.

I am always amazed when I meet people, especially young people, around the world by their idealism, by their sense that this world is meant to be a lot better than it is, by the commitment they have for things like the green movement, peace, working against injustice and oppression. And they are right, because God's will for us is a world that is hospitable to goodness, to laughter, to joy, to compassion, to caring, for a world where people matter more than things, matter more than profits. And there are moments when we glimpse that kind of world.

There are many people who face some of the most horrendous circumstances with incredible courage. I often go out to where people hurt – the ghettos and settlements – thinking I am going to minister to them but almost always they minister to me. Their resilience – their capacity to laugh in those circumstances – lifts me. I wonder how I would survive in their situation, but they don't let that get them down. Human beings are incredible; they have an enormous capacity for evil, but they also have a remarkable capacity for good. And that is what is about to explode in our world.

It takes no special sensitivity to realise how pervasive is the stress and violence to which the fabric of our contemporary world is subjected. And yet violence is not the substance, it is the symptom. Something new is waiting to be born. We are experiencing the sacred moment of the birth pangs of a new age, of a new hope. What struggles to arise out of the past might become our shared future of mutual hearing and understanding, of an unprecedented willingness to acknowledge and accept others in all their difference. Will we recognise the miracle of this possibility? Are we willing to help it be pulled into the light of tomorrow? These are not merely questions. They are the agenda of tomorrow. They are the path towards a leap of faith with one another that will move humanity and our earth into a new era of reconciliation and hope.

2

*W*HY STOP NOW?

Susan George

Far be it from me to take issue with the organisers of the multi-dimensional and multi-media cultural event which is *The Right to Hope*, but the carper in me (and the erstwhile philosophy student) immediately needs to scrutinise their chosen title. No writer believes that words are innocent and I want to ask why the terms 'right' and 'hope' should be juxtaposed.

What is a 'right' if not an additional human freedom achieved, usually after a long and frequently bloody struggle by a determined minority; usually then codified and enshrined in national or international law; all too often called into question by those who perceive that the hard-won right is contrary to their interests?

It took the world's first anti-colonial revolution to establish the Bill of Rights attached to the Constitution of the United States. Much subsequent US history has witnessed attempts to water it down, for example those of the present-day gun lobby with its systematic distortions of the 'right to bear arms'. One of the first acts of the French revolutionaries was to proclaim the Rights of Man and the Citizen – but they had to behead the reigning monarchs and displace an entire ruling class to make it stick. The UN's Universal Declaration of Human Rights is honoured mostly in the breach and the most fundamental among them – the right not to be slaughtered – has been violated with increasing frequency in our own time as the 'international community' has discreetly looked the other way.

I believe that hope *allows* people to struggle for rights, to create, to affirm their dignity. Fortunately for us all, hope is coextensive with the human condition, not an elusive goal to be constantly beaten back yet constantly reaffirmed. Hope is what makes politics possible: collective hope, far more than collective despair, has been at the root of every significant change in human history. Let us understand hope as a virtue, in the Christian sense, or as one of the distinguishing natural and moral attributes which differentiates human beings from other creatures. Thus understood, we shall fully affirm its transforming power. In these troubled times, we have enough to fight against, and to fight for, without having to fight for hope as well!

This point clarified, I can readily understand why those who conceived this event chose their title. Perhaps one's own particular present has always seemed to those living it the worst of all possible times, indeed a 'hopeless' time. Still, our own era strikes me as a worthy rival for all other existing candidates (including the 14th century). The four horsemen of the apocalyptic tradition are now accompanied by a fifth terrible rider who bears the news of the serious possibility of the extinction of the human species.

To the catalogue of ills other times and other civilisations have been forced to confront, we can now add the wanton destruction of the natural base which sustains life – though scientists suspect that pests like crows, flies, mosquitoes, cockroaches and similar wide-ranging species are capable of adaptation to vastly altered ecological circumstances, which is scant consolation. Finitude and death close in upon not just the individual, the family, even upon peoples, but also upon the evolutionary experiment we call humanity.

If Spinoza was right, the first natural postulate is that all beings desire to persevere in their being. If Aristotle was right, man is a rational animal. For the individual being, for the individual man, fair enough. The question is, rather, whether social aggregates of beings and collective 'man' necessarily boast the same attributes. Our present array of survival mechanisms strongly suggest that they do not.

By accident or by design, our global economic machinery now virtually guarantees the destruction of viable societies in the mid- to longer term. Every society *has* an economy – which can be defined as a set of arrangements and enforced rules for acquiring or producing material goods and services which sustain individual and community life. It does not follow that a society *is*, or should be, first and foremost an economy. For centuries, society encompassed and superseded the economy. Whatever 'arrangements and enforced rules' were chosen (some of them quite horrible ones, as in slave-based systems) they were put in place for social, cultural and political reasons, not purely economic ones.

The economic doctrine now espoused and the economic arrangements now adopted worldwide, particularly over the past two decades, benefit a smaller and smaller minority of the planet's inhabitants while excluding the majority. This is not a moral judgement but a factual statement, supported by overwhelming evidence showing increased concentration of wealth in fewer and fewer hands. According to the UNDP, the richest 20 per cent of humanity now control 85 per cent of the world's wealth, while the bottom 20 per cent must make do with a mere 1.4 per cent of that wealth. One striking example, though not a 'scientific' one because it does not compare like categories, is the existence of 358 billionaires, with a combined economic worth estimated by *Forbes* magazine at $760 billion. This makes those 358 individuals roughly equivalent, economically speaking, to nearly two billion people whose annual share of GNP, according to World Bank figures, is $390.

The phenomenon holds for income distribution within countries, including advanced ones like Britain and the United States, as well as between rich and poor nations. Everywhere the rich grow richer and the poor are robbed of what little they have. Such disparities are the logical outcome of a system which allows the 'free' market to make most of our decisions for us and this system has penetrated the entire world. Global markets, assumed to be self-regulating, exist for finance (investment or speculative capital), labour and natural resources as well as for the usual goods and services. By definition, the market understands only the language of money and cannot register the needs of those who have little or no purchasing power. Yet it has been elevated to the status of a quasi-natural law which assumes that human motivation can be reduced to the desire for accumulation and profit, that human beings will work only because starvation is the alternative.

Although the market can perform many useful services and can contribute to making societies wealthier and healthier, no one should ask it to do what it was never designed to do. It cannot, in particular, provide jobs for everyone – jobs are at best a by-product of its functioning. Paradoxically, if we want to retain the benefits of the market, then it must be controlled and regulated through international structures and agreed processes which prevent it from carrying inequalities to such extremes that society, and the natural base on which it rests, will self-destruct and take us all along with it.

Unfortunately, the major international institutions now in place do not consider market regulation their mandate – quite the contrary. The World Bank, the International Monetary Fund, and the new World Trade Organisation are all bent on further deregulation and on increasing the dependency of all countries on the global marketplace. Huge and unpayable debts have forced dozens of countries to concentrate their efforts on hard currency-earning exports to the detriment of investment toward the satisfaction of local needs. Through structural adjustment programmes, the World Bank and the IMF have weakened the capacity of individual governments to protect their citizens against the harmful effects of the market.

'Free' (deregulated) trade between unequals promotes the survival of the fittest. The African peasant, for example, cannot hope to compete against the farmer from Iowa or East Anglia (both of them indirectly subsidised besides, in defiance of normal 'free' market rules). Deregulated or 'free' investment seeks out those countries which are prepared to pay the lowest wages and impose the lowest standards for safety, health, environmental protection and the like. Although the investments of transnational corporations in the so-called 'Third World' had by 1994 created twelve million jobs, half of those jobs were in China. The number of jobs destroyed locally by these transnationals is never calculated in the available statistics.

The famous doctrine of Comparative Advantage works only so long as capital remains national. Once denationalised, comparative advantage gives way to *absolute* advantage as countries vie with each other to attract investment, whatever the consequences for workers and the environment. Thus the global marketplace rewards choices which are the most socially and environmentally irresponsible, in a constant 'race to the bottom', even though those choices may be the most economically profitable in the short term. Society at large is expected to pay the bill for the 'side-effects' of the market's functioning, but finds itself increasingly less able to do so.

Perhaps the most dangerous and least noticed failing of the market is its utter inability to tell us what we need to know before disaster strikes. This became clear in the financial arena with the Mexican crisis of late 1994 and early 1995 when panicky investors fought to remove their money from a country touted only weeks before as one of the great economic success stories of the decade. Almost immediately, three-quarters of a million jobs disappeared and further loss of employment and lowering of the standard of living for ordinary Mexicans lie ahead.

The market is completely ignorant of ecology and tells us nothing about exhausted land, overfished waters or decimated forests. So long as they last, the food, the fish, the trees are counted as income, with no notice at all taken of the depletion of natural capital which will soon make it impossible to produce further food, fish or trees. No 'costs' in the accounting sense are registered, only revenues and profits. An entrepreneur who spent down his capital in this manner would soon find himself bankrupt, but in our current system, natural resources are being squandered, with predictable consequences.

Nor can the market provide us with useful information about the consequences of industrial processes, particularly the accumulation of pollutants in the land, water and air or the emissions of CO_2 and other greenhouse gases in the atmosphere. If climate change on the scale now predicted by many experts does occur, the costs – including the economic costs – will be infinite, but the market will give no warning when we have gone too far, as may well be the case already.

The tableau is indeed grim and the individual has rarely seemed, or felt, so powerless faced with the immensity and the acceleration of supra-national forces arrayed against him or her – so where does hope come in, if indeed it does?

The works of art displayed in *The Right to Hope* exhibit are in themselves sufficient proof that the human spirit is alive and well, but there are many other objective reasons besides enduring individual creativity to place our trust in the future.

Our present market-based system, although globalised and elevated to near religious status, is in fact an aberration in human history. As Karl Polanyi has shown (in *The Great Transformation*, 1944, and other works), this system arose during the Industrial Revolution in mid-19th century England. Nowhere else and at no other time had the self-regulating market been enshrined as the dominant principle of economic and social organisation; nowhere else and at no other time had money, human labour and nature itself all been treated as commodities and subjected to the laws of supply and demand.

Polanyi also showed how, left to its own devices, the self-regulating market system would have destroyed society. Recognising this implicitly or explicitly, 19th century England undertook to proect itself. From all political quarters – left, right and centre – as the signs of social destruction accumulated, reformers and reforms arose to shield the community against the market's destructive power. The rise of the market and of regulation were simultaneous phenomena.

The task of the late 20th century is, granted, a far more difficult one because it requires regulation not just in one country, but worldwide; even so, this should not be an insuperable obstacle. The cracks in the system (eg Mexico) are showing and even those who benefit most from it may well decide that regulation is in their ultimate interest and preferable to exposing themselves to further shocks. The Bretton Woods Institutions (the World Bank and the IMF) have been subjected to unrelenting criticism from a host of non-governmental organisations united in the *50 Years is Enough* campaign, and there are signs that they will eventually be obliged to make internal changes.

The UN Conference on Environment and Development in Rio in 1992 seems to have hampered more than helped the environmental movement. In Rio, the transnational corporations were omnipresent and affirmed their right to self-regulation. But it is only a matter of time before this movement is reinvigorated – nature will provide the wake-up calls that no amount of rhetoric can stifle. In early May 1995, high-level representatives of nine major world religions, in a new stage of expressing their concern for the earth, will announce the nine-year conservation strategies that each will convey to its own faithful.

What's more, the technology already exists to make our human presence less burdensome to the planet. The insurance industry is pushing hard for solar energy to replace greenhouse gas-producing fossil fuels. Major insurers now employ their own climatologists because over the past decade they have had to pay out an unprecedented $50 billion in climate-related disasters (tropical storms and floods). Here is a major source of pressure within the world of business – and even the oil lobby cannot hold out forever.

Most of all, perhaps, hope is warranted because throughout the world, thousands upon thousands of citizens' groups are springing up. They may not always be recognisable as classic NGOs; sometimes they are devoted to a single interest or local objective, but their common feature is refusal of the *status quo*. They are increasingly linked through real-time electronic communications so that a worldwide protest, or project, can be mounted in a matter of hours. This worldwide mobilisation is perhaps the great unreported story of the end of the 20th century. When citizens realise their collective strengths and begin to capitalise on it, they will be unstoppable.

If hope is not, as I believe it is not, a right; if it is not a duty either, then what is it? I can only define it as a way of living honourably and with dignity to improve the human condition in the historical circumstances of one's own time, however hard those circumstances. This is what our ancestors did – that is why we are here – producing exhibits and films and books – not living in caves. Why stop now?

3

BOTTLENECKS OF DEVELOPMENT

Wangari Maathai

The United Nations celebrates its fiftieth anniversary in 1995. Many acknowledge that the UN is the global body around which the people of the world and their governments should rally, and are producing reports on where the UN should go in the next fifty years, and what type of UN it should be in a world so different from the one of 1945. Africa draws particular concern. In 1945 the continent was largely divided between the great European powers; it is now free but still largely unable to catch up with the rest of the world in almost all areas, thereby risking complete marginalisation. For that reason, it is acknowledged that Africa deserves special attention compared with, for example, some of the former colonies in Asia and South America which also shared the colonial legacy and, along with Africa, started on about the same economic footing.

In the course of my work with the Green Belt Movement, I have identified what I have come to call 'bottlenecks of development' and, while I have based my observations and experiences in Kenya, many of them are applicable to other countries, especially in sub-Saharan Africa.

The Green Belt Movement is an indigenous, grassroots, environmental and developmental non-governmental organisation (NGO), whose main activity is tree planting and whose membership is mainly rural women. It has identified both short- and long-term objectives which it pursues concurrently. Our overall objective has been to raise public awareness of the need to rehabilitate and protect the environment, especially through tree planting. Another of our long-term objectives is to make development a participatory process which empowers people to address not only the symptoms of environmental degradation, but also its causes. It is easier to articulate those objectives than to realise them.

Some three decades ago, the political leaders of post-war Africa had three major objectives in mind as they became the first post-colonial African rulers: to oversee the decolonisation of the entire continent, to promote African unity, and to effect economic development. Kwame Nkrumah of Ghana urged his peers to seek first political freedom and all else would follow.

With the recent political freedom of Namibia and South Africa, that generation of African leaders may consider their first agenda complete. But, as they knew only too well, decolonising territories is only the first step. African unity and economic development have completely eluded the subsequent generation of African leaders, who largely became dictatorial chieftains of their now impoverished and collapsing states. They have been unable to free their people from insecurity, poverty, ignorance and indignity. That is partly because 500 years is a long time to struggle against oppression. The battles of five centuries have left Africans weakened culturally, economically and politically. An even more difficult task will be the cultural decolonisation of the African mind. The world cannot ignore centuries of cultural adulteration of the African people through religious and intellectual indoctrination against their heritage; this adulteration is still going on.

It is important to recognise the processes through which African people have become disengaged and disempowered. Otherwise, we perpetuate the legacy of blaming the victim. Of course, the slave trade was a gross violation of the African people, and they are still struggling under its negative psychological and economic impact. Neo-colonialism continues to treat Africa as a market for finished industrial goods, while encouraging the continent's peoples to continue producing stimulants for a non-sympathetic world market on which she has no impact.

However, this must not be an excuse of the African people for a perpetual litany of woes about colonialism, slavery and other injustices against them. Indeed, this is part of their heritage. These gross violations of the rights of the African peoples should be living examples of the many battles they have fought and won. They are valiant examples of where the power of evil has been overcome by the power of good. Like the Wailing Wall of Jerusalem, these struggles should be symbols of the power of the human spirit. They should be a source of pride, inspiration and hope for all who seek good from human spirituality. A people less endowed would have become extinct and long forgotten. This rich heritage should be used not to disempower the African people and create a handicap for them, but, instead, should be a source of their empowerment, rather than the reason to keep them on the back stage of their own political and economic agenda.

Such steps are often only carried out by visionary leaders who have the political will to invest in the social, political and economic well-being of their people. In Africa, this type of leader has not yet wholly emerged. Leadership in Africa has been more concerned with the opportunity to control the State and all its resources. Such leadership seeks the power, prestige and comfortable lifestyles that the national resources can support. It is the sort of leadership that has built armies and security networks to protect itself against its own citizens. With the new wave of popular desire for democratic governance and for more freedom, ethnic nationalism is being encouraged by such leaders in a desperate move to hold onto power. With this type of leadership in place it is difficult to help Africa.

The problems unfolding on the continent are not caused by 'fate'. They are the inevitable consequences of the mistakes which have been made in the past. Furthermore, trying to stitch the pieces together without understanding the forces which tore the continent apart will address only part of the problem and provide only part of the solution.

For example, people conveniently forget that, prior to the 'discovery' of Africa, many African 'states' were governing themselves through unwritten constitutions which ensured peace, liberty and prosperity, resulting in a feeling of happiness and self-fulfilment. It is in part the countries which exploited Africa who contributed to the distorted picture of an Africa at war with itself. This was done deliberately because it justified intervention, slavery and colonialism with the accompanying benefits.

Without an indigenous art of literacy, and lacking in technological advances to put the record straight, Africans have been unable to correct the distortions paraded as truths so often and for so long – even the victims have begun to accept them as truths. One such deception is that good governance did not exist in pre-colonial Africa and, therefore, democracy is a Western value now being exported to Africa. I can state categorically that my own Kikuyu community had a pre-colonial democratic governance which rivalled any in the world today.

So how do we go about facing our current challenges and playing our role to free the African people from insecurity, ignorance and disease? This is the question our post-war and even post-colonial leaders asked themselves. It seems like the question the UN is asking itself. I have, therefore, decided to spend time looking for answers. To me, the first answer is to identify the bottlenecks which frustrate the efforts being made. Perhaps none of the bottlenecks mentioned below is new, but I believe they have to be addressed if we genuinely want to help Africa. They continue to be raised because I believe that without understanding these bottlenecks, friends of Africa will continue to address the symptoms rather than the causes of the continent's problems. Some of these I have identified in the course of my work

with the Green Belt Movement and they are as follows:

1. Development is still not human-centred, not participatory, and not for the people and by the people

Development efforts continue to keep the majority of the African people in the back stage of their development and political agenda. It appears that the successes we have registered with the Green Belt Movement are to a large measure due to the fact that our approach to develop is participatory and bottom-up. It has no blueprint, preferring to rely on a trial-and-error method using the expertise, knowledge and the capability of the local people. It addresses both the symptoms and the causes of environmental degradation. It adapts what seems to work and quickly drops what does not. It prioritises on meeting the felt needs of communities: creating jobs, improving the economic status of women, transferring farming techniques and tools, providing woodfuel for rural populations and the urban poor, fighting malnutrition, especially by planting fruit trees and indigenous food crops, providing fencing and building materials and protecting forests, water catchment areas and open spaces in urban centres.

2. International debt

The African international debt should be forgiven, with the understanding that those in power will not rush out to borrow more at the level of their previous borrowing. In future such borrowing should be public and the responsibility should be held by more mechanisms of governance than just the individuals in the government of the day. Forgiving debts of governments which are not transparent, accountable and responsible to their people would not solve any problems; no sooner is the debt forgiven than the leaders rush to international donors to borrow more on behalf of the people, but continue to mismanage it without the knowledge of the people.

3. Style of leadership

The style of leadership is another reason why human-centred development has been ignored. Dictatorial leaders who were unpopular with their citizens received huge military aid and built up massive armies, police forces and an equally huge network of secret service agencies whose main preoccupation was, and still is, to spy on their own citizens. Yet hardly any African country has gone to war with its neighbour. Most wars and conflicts are internal.

In many African states, including the one I know best, Kenya, citizens have become prisoners within their own borders. The preoccupation with internal security and political survival by leaders encourages the misapplication of scarce resources and the sacrifice of any agenda for development. It also encourages leaders to make changes in national constitutions to grant themselves absolute powers and control over all national resources and mechanisms of governance (such as radio, television, the judicial system, the armed forces and the civil service, especially the local chiefs and headmen).

These instruments, originally intended to provide checks and balances and prevent dictatorial tendencies, are manipulated or censored to ensure that the leaders stay in power and enjoy the privileges these instruments control. So poised, many of the current African leaders enjoy immense power and control and indeed run states as if they were their own personal property. They have invented divisive and manipulative tactics, such as the ongoing politically-motivated tribal clashes in Kenya, in order to stay in power. Since freedom of the press and dissemination of information is curtailed, citizens are not allowed to assemble, associate or move freely without being harassed by armed policemen. It is difficult to empower people so that they can liberate themselves from their own leaders.

That is why dictators will continue to argue that democracy is a Western value which cannot work in Africa. But, at the same time, they deny citizens the right to civil education, political assemblies and constitutional conventions to decide for themselves what type of democracy they want.

That is also the reason why the democratisation process is being frustrated. Africans, like all other human beings, want justice, equity, transparency, responsibility and accountability. They want respect and human dignity. They want a decent quality of life and an opportunity to feed, shelter and clothe their families. They are not seeking to dominate or marginalise each other. They want to create a strong civil society which can hold its leaders accountable and responsible, as well as sustain mechanisms of governance which ensure the security of the people, rather than the security of heads of states and the small group of supporters and political opportunists who surround them.

As we look at such a bottleneck, it would appear that Kwame Nkrumah was right. Only, he did not underline that political freedom must be grounded in liberty, justice and equality. The recent power-sharing in South Africa offers an alternative for Africa. There, the political culture of 'the winner takes all' is forfeited for national unity.

4. *The environment is neglected and mismanaged*

The environment is neglected despite the political statements at national and international levels. The only reason why the Green Belt Movement is vilified by the government is that it has criticised government action (or even lack of action) for the environment. Currently, for example, the Ministers of Environment and Natural Resources and of Lands have permitted encroachment on many indigenous forests, to give land plots to political supporters. For political expediency and opportunism, they are thereby sacrificing environmental national interests, like water catchment areas and bio-diversity in indigenous forests. They have allowed the grabbing of most open spaces in Kenyan cities and urban centres. These are given out to rich individuals and communities in return for the financial contributions they give to leaders. Instead of the authorities developing open spaces and parks for a better quality of life in the urban centres, they use them to entrench themselves in power.

To address adequately such environmental issues, the Green Belt Movement is forced also to address the economic and political reasons for such actions, because there is an important linkage between a non-accountable and non-transparent governance, and environmental mismanagement. It is, therefore, impossible to protect the environment unless there is a government which is accountable to its people.

5. *The absence of peace and security in Africa*

All human beings aspire to, and deserve, peace and security, which are prerequisites to human development. In 1945, the UN was formed to ensure that future wars and the misery they bring would be avoided. But since independence, many African states have hardly enjoyed internal peace and security, because the post-colonial leaders digressed from their initial vision and became dictatorial and oppressive.

The euphoria generated by the end of colonialism, freedom, and independence, was gradually replaced by a culture of fear and silence as the people became ostracised by their leaders. The geo-political rivalry of the superpowers during the Cold War became a reason why oppressive systems of governance flourished in Africa. The outcry of citizens in many countries over the gross violations of human rights went unhindered until the Cold War was over. Dictators were presented as benevolent leaders and their nations were portrayed as peaceful, secure and prosperous. But those were the days of the Cold War and misrepresentation was part of the War. In Africa,

therefore, the Cold War precipitated some of the most devastating internal wars, as African friends and foes of the superpowers fought for economic and political control. It also justified political and economic oppression and violation of human rights in many countries – a trend, by the way, which has not ceased with the end of the Cold War. But, especially during the Cold War, human and material resources were diverted towards international wars, conflicts and internal security of state governors, rather than towards human development. Funds were used to purchase weaponry used to suppress dissidents and popular movements.

6. *International cooperation for a truly human development is still lacking*

Africa is still being marginalised. There is lack of genuine support and cooperation from the rich international community, notwithstanding the rhetoric at international forums. The international community is not ignorant of the problems facing the African people, because they are discussed in a myriad of books, magazines, evaluation reports and development plans, many of which are written by experts from the same communities. Nevertheless, much of the foreign aid comes in the form of curative social welfare programmes, such as famine relief, food aid, population control programmes, assistance to refugees and support of peace-keeping forces and humanitarian missions.

Resources are hardly available if they are needed for preventive and sustainable human development programmes such as education, training, building of infrastructures, enhancing the capacity of institutions, promoting food production and processing at the local level and for local consumption, promotion of entrepreneurship and development of cultural and social programmes which empower people so that they can tap their creative energies and capacities.

7. *Corruption*

While corruption is a worldwide crime, it reaches devastating proportions in Africa because it is coupled with undemocratic and, therefore, unaccountable and non-transparent leadership which cannot be held responsible by its people. It is suggested that funds which are advanced to Africa for development are stolen and stashed away in secret bank accounts in developed countries.

Much secrecy surrounds these financial transactions, but it is claimed that if these funds were made available to Africa, she would need no more aid and we would not hear of a phenomenon now being referred to as 'donor fatigue'. So why can't these funds be located and returned to the World Bank and IMF or whoever had advanced them to the African leaders, to help get rid of the international debts? This would be a case of retrieving stolen capital and returning it to the original owner! This would relieve millions of debt-ridden Africans from responsibilities their leaders unjustly bound them to. It is a matter of ethics: a matter of being just and fair to ordinary Africans on whose behalf the funds were borrowed and from whom the World Bank and IMF demand repayment through crippling structural adjustment programmes. Many future generations of Africans will still be born already deeply in debt unless this matter is addressed. When the truth about these financial transactions is finally exposed, we shall be as shocked as the world was when we comprehended the atrocities of the slave trade or the holocaust.

If it is a crime to kill thousands of people in Kashmir, Yugoslavia or Rwanda, it should be a crime to steal millions of dollars from the people and thereby cause death indirectly to innocent millions through hunger, malnutrition, lack of adequate health care and inflationary prices, which make it impossible to provide basic needs. Concern for Africa (and for other regions in similar predicaments) ought to be concern for the African people and

for the future generations of Africans. Those who cooperate and protect stolen wealth should not be protected by global public opinion which wishes to pretend that this is the way Africa does business. Perhaps it is time there was a global ethic or a code of moral responsibility to cite corruption as a threat to peace and security.

8. *Developing a market which benefits Africa*

Despite many countries having achieved political independence, the economic market is still designed to supply mainly stimulants like coffee, tea and cocoa and luxury delicacies like nuts, beans, tropical fruits and flowers. International investments are important and an open market is desired. Many countries have their markets laid bare for international investments, and especially under the economic direction of international financial institutions.

However, unless one has a government which cares about its people and protects them from external exploitation, it is difficult to see how any development model designed and carried out by an international community which comes to make profits would generate wealth for the African people. And none has. The continent is wealthy, but the wealth is mined by, and for the benefit of, others outside the region. Of course, it is her leaders who facilitate this mining of the wealth from the continent to other regions, but that does not make it fair and just.

9. *Poverty, poor health and sustained hunger*

Good health is essential for sustained, creative and productive work and life. Healthy individuals are resourceful and creative and have the urge to fulfil their full potential. If millions of people never have enough to eat, are undernourished and are suffering from parasitic infestations and diseases associated with malnutrition and poor sanitation, development is bound to stagnate. Poverty, poor health and sustained hunger become a vicious, endless circle of misery and want.

Notwithstanding statements at international conferences and round tables of development agencies about agriculture, food security, farming techniques and preventive medicine, the only farming sector which receives adequate attention is that which brings in foreign exchange. Food has become a political weapon with the leaders in power holding the key to the national granaries, disposing of the food even when their own people need it, and subsequently appealing for food from the international community. The national agricultural policies discourage local farmers and opt for cheap food from the international community.

Most of the available food is produced by women, who also carry much of the burden for work done in the rural areas at a family level. But women's work is still rated low, is hardly rewarded, and has no prestige. Agriculture and food production in Africa are still relegated to poorly educated rural people. In this area, again, it is only a government that cares about its people which will protect its citizens from the politics of food. And only an informed, strong civil society could persuade or force its government not to sacrifice the local farmers at the altar of international food politics.

Africa has a fragile environment and experiences frequent droughts and insufficient rains. Famines can be prevented by efficient planning by a leadership which puts its people first. UN agencies and donor communities will help and supplement, but it is impossible for outsiders to rush to Africa and make urgent plans where the leaders have failed to live up to their responsibilities.

10. Illiteracy and ignorance

Yet another obstacle to development is illiteracy and ignorance. The older generation of illiterate people were persuaded to overvalue education and the ability to read and write. They equated this type of education with progress and a ticket for instant escape from poverty. Certificates of education are seen as passports to white-collar jobs and instant wealth. The ordinary people trust too readily those who can read and write and those with degrees and certificates of achievement. And, at the same time, they tend to undervalue and underestimate themselves. Unfortunately, those who have these qualifications often live and behave as if they have the ticket to escape not only poverty, but also hard work, honesty and responsibility.

Therefore, while this self-undervaluation puts many ordinary people at the mercy of literate members of the community and the state-controlled mass media, they are also taken advantage of and exploited by their own people who ought to rescue them! In many countries, the national radio and television are the main means of communication and are intended for public education and information dissemination. Many leaders not only use the national radio and television for political propaganda and personal aggrandisement, but fail to invest resources into education.

11. Foreign languages form a communication barrier

Literacy, language, culture and investment in human resources, especially in formal education, are important for development. None of the developed countries or recently developing regions has been as eroded, especially culturally, linguistically and religiously, as Africa tends to be.

At independence, many African states adopted foreign languages. Education is often equated with the ability to speak and write these languages and entry into the job market is virtually impossible without the ability to read and write in them. But only a small number of the élite speak and write these languages fluently.

In a continent where illiteracy is very high, communication technology sparse, transport slow and inadequate, use of foreign languages marginalises a majority of the indigenous populations and greatly reduces their capacity to play a meaningful role in the political and economic life of their country. Leaders and the small number of middle class élite who control the life of the nation speak to each other and bypass the majority of the public.

The inability of a country to communicate effectively with itself ought to be recognised as a major obstacle to development, especially at this time of communication revolution. Fear of losing power and losing the grip leaders have on their people is one of the reasons local people are discouraged from using their mother tongues. The only book which is freely translated into local languages is the Bible!

Even then, the inability to communicate effectively disempowers people, kills their self-confidence and destroys creative energy. It also minimises indigenous knowledge and expertise, especially in Africa where none of it is written in an indigenous artform. It will take courage to admit that languages so highly valued in the world may not be essential for all of the half a billion Africans and may in fact be a bottleneck to their development. Insisting on foreign languages for universal functional literacy and in information dissemination in Africa is the surest way of keeping Africa illiterate, ignorant and uninformed.

12. Inability to catch up with modern science and technology

Scientific knowledge and creative innovations are lacking in our educational system where technological creativity is not given deliberate priority and incentives. Technology transfer is reduced to basic training for consumers of

technological imported goods. As a result, information, manufacturing and assembling industries are still in their infancy. No doubt there is injustice in trade, but without scientific and technological development, Africa is easily marginalised from global communications and economy.

13. *The rapid increase in population and low income*

When tragedies like famine and civil wars hit Africa, a high rate of population increase is blamed. Rarely do people compare consumption patterns of the developed countries with the populations in those countries. But they are two sides of the same coin. In a just world, those over-consuming the world's resources would have to adjust their quality of life, rather than continue the exploitation of other people's resources. This would allow others to get something too. Blaming the numbers in the poorest regions of the world is to tell only half the story.

14. *Spirituality*

Spiritually, Africa looks for inspiration from the Christian and Islamic worlds. None of the spiritual experiences of Africa has been given attention, because none of them is coded in scriptural writings associated with prophets and holy men. The indigenous spiritual heritage of many Africans has largely been relegated to primitive expression more akin to the unholy dark world of the evil spirits and the devil. To many African devotees of Christianity and Islam, seeking African spiritual heritage is devil worship. To many other people, seeking African roots, once condemned and overwhelmed by foreign cultures, is a fulfilling experience.

As a result, much of the African traditional wisdom and cultural heritage has been destroyed. Indeed, Africans have been encouraged to be ashamed of their heritage and to ape foreign cultures and values, much to their detriment.

People who are robbed of their heritage during occupation, enslavement and political and religious colonisation, become disorientated and disempowered. They lose self-respect and self-confidence as well as the capacity for self-guidance, leadership and independent decision-making. Kenyans are today worried about devil worship. Yet the constitution guarantees the freedom of worship. At the same time, a group of individuals who have tried to reintroduce the form of worship of their forefathers has been declared an illegal assembly. The freedom of worship is therefore only guaranteed to people who accept foreign faiths. It is easy to appreciate why the colonial government would have prevented indigenous forms of worship so that the natives could be more easily converted to the religion of the master, but it is astonishing that African leaders should deny freedom of worship to indigenous people.

All human beings have their traditional culture, knowledge, wisdom, and values. These have been accumulated over thousands of years. They have been passed from one generation to another. This accumulated heritage directs communities in times of peace or insecurity, and in times of birth, life and death. It is their antennae into the unknown future and their reference point into their past. While some peoples have invented the art of reading and writing and have been able to record their accumulated knowledge and wisdom, others pass it on through oral instructions, stories, ceremonies, and customs.

When this rich heritage is used to disempower the African people, it becomes a bottleneck of development when it should be the source of our empowerment, of hope.

4

Bringing the World to Bear: Media, Culture and Development

Adrian Cleasby

There is a deeply rooted, vexed and essentially ethical question about how important the media has become in the move towards sustainable, inclusive and culturally appropriate patterns of development. Perhaps a good way to start unravelling the knot is to think of a land you have never been to, or a community you have never encountered, then ask yourself, 'Whatever I know about this place, about these people, how did that knowledge come to me?'

Any thoughts about cross-cultural communication, including those expressed with such lucidity and embodied so beautifully elsewhere within *The Right to Hope*, must make use of – and so make sense of – the mass media. If understanding anything is finding order in it, making sense of the media is no easy task. The collective noun denotes a mass of people, organisations and technologies and, equally significantly, *connotes* the scattered, disparate, apparently chaotic jumble of images, words, signs, propaganda and perspectives they produce. Some of these are stamped boldly in print in the book you are holding now, or in your daily newspaper. Some are hurtling digitally along cables on the other side of the world and some are surging invisibly through the atmosphere at the speed of light, through you and around you, weaving an ever-shifting web of electro-magnetic energy round the earth, only to pop up as pictures on your TV set or voices on your radio.

For Good or Ill

At its best, the media can transcend physical and ideological boundaries, spanning oceans, nations and history to offer us surrogate experiences of life in areas where we have no first-hand knowledge, to consolidate our understanding of areas where we do and to force us to reassess our stereotypes and muddle-headed notions. It can bring the world to bear with an immediacy and intimacy which our generations have been the first to witness. Nelson Mandela has credited a worldwide media iconography as a powerful catalyst in the erosion of apartheid and increasingly commentators note how many of us, previously without voice, are now finding ways to empowerment through communion with cultures, thinkers and activists which new technologies and participatory media make ever more accessible.

At its worst, we know too well how profound the power of the media can be. How, before and during the genocide in Rwanda, for instance, the radio station *Milles Collines* poured hours of racist propaganda out across the airwaves, exacerbating and goading the massacre of innocent citizens, inciting a nation to slaughter its own.

The Reverend Desmond Tutu has spoken of the complementarity of nations as a metaphor for all humanity of our need of one another. If the fault-lines between and within civilisations are not to erupt as the battle-lines of an intolerant and hopeless future, then the media has a profound role to play in dispelling the fear, mistrust and loathing which

ignorance and alienation breed. The choice is ours – each and every one. We can sit back, give up and switch off while our increasingly mediated future unravels any which way, for good or indescribable ill. We can be a thoughtless, docile herd grazing on entertainment and advertising. Or we can develop our critical disposition, our longing for wisdom and, above all else, earn our right to hope as we engage in the Global Media Debate.

Television as a Touchstone

Blatant propaganda is one thing. More often the media shores up our ignorance inadvertently, as recent trends in television may serve to illustrate. Of all the means of mass communication, increasingly television is the way in which the world recognises and talks to itself. In 1965, according to BBC estimates, there were around 180 million TV sets in the world. By 1990 there were more than a billion. UNESCO sources have estimated that across the African continent there are now more than 16 times the number of TV sets per thousand people than there were 20 years ago. In America there are something like 800 TV sets per 1000 people. And in the United Kingdom, public opinion surveys indicate that an overwhelming 82 per cent of the population cite television as their primary source of information about world affairs.

Television programmes have an extraordinary capacity to bring into sharp, visual and (to all appearances) immediate relief the lives, experiences and environments of people from places in the world, or within our own society, that we may never meet face to face. They can fire our imagination and sense of wonder at what life might be like for the subject of a programme and this wonderful leap of faith, this ability to imagine the world as others see it, is an essential part of what makes us human. In this respect, programme-makers are closely akin to artists and myth-makers. Yet across the world there are signs that media managers have no clear sense of the lead the programme-makers can provide nor the good they can promote.

Crisis Point

It may be symptomatic of a world in crisis that, for many societies, issues close to home seem suddenly more pressing, more complex and more *demanding* than ever before. Under the mounting pressures of free-market economics, media organisations have two broad responses to the resulting shift in demand; they offer audiences more material of relevance to their everyday lives and more light relief from what Mary Midgley has described here as 'the exhausting business of confronting reality'.

The two are not mutually exclusive – we often see examples of both in the same evening's viewing and there is a place for each. Unfortunately, the 'relevant' programmes frequently turn out to be parochial, insular and alienating, while the 'light relief' is often mindless trivia or sheer exotica, so far removed from local concerns that it objectifies and distances the world it portrays.

As we become less well-informed about one another's predicament, so we feel less involved. As we see less and less of the underlying causes of, or practical solutions to, global poverty and environmental degradation, so popular pressure for serious political change fizzles out. And then, as if inexplicably, we sense the global crisis deepening.

The UK Experience

The trend towards parochial broadcasting is particularly apparent in the UK. British-based organisations like the BBC, Channel Four and ITV enjoy a worldwide reputation for the quality and editorial integrity of their coverage of international affairs. As producers, these outfits have a significance which outweighs their size since their programmes are carried by so many broadcasters around the world. The BBC's Developing Stories, for example, a series co-produced by Television Trust for the Environment (TVE) and shown originally as part of the One World initiative, has introduced the work of some of the most outstanding film-makers in the South to countless millions of viewers in over a hundred countries and won scores of international awards.

Yet on the domestic front, such broader world perspectives are being sidelined by programmes which, in the words of the BBC, 'address the interests and priorities of our audience and include more news and analysis of immediate relevance to them.'(Yentob, A and Forgan, E (1995) *People and Programmes*) What is 'immediately relevant' to the UK audience? Not, apparently *Developing Stories*, which the BBC has dropped from its schedule. Instead it is giving more and more air-time to 'stories, ideas and trends in the UK' and senior managers offer lists of programmes which 'now have an explicit brief to report the UK more comprehensively.'(Yentob, A and Forgan, E, ibid) This line of thinking is not peculiar to the BBC but the key question it raises is whether anything can be *comprehensively* reported, described or understood if it is seen only *in isolation from its broader context*.

There is a very real danger that such a narrow definition of 'immediate relevance' may well be self-fulfilling. The UK's then Independent Broadcasting Authority (IBA) carried out research in 1987 which clearly showed that 'the more that people see of countries on television, whether they are Third World or non-Third World members, the more that people think events in those countries affect Britain.' (Wober, J M (1987) *TV and the Third World* – A British View, IBA.)

So, sustained coverage seems to stimulate audiences into thinking about the connectedness of their lives with people who are, at first glance, very far removed and there is no reason to suspect that UK audiences are peculiar in this respect. The IBA pointed out an uncomplicated truth but the BBC's recent programme strategy suggests things are working exactly the opposite way around in contemporary Britain.

The surge in UK-centric programming has resulted in a rapid decline of in-depth perspectives on the rest of the world, especially of Southern countries. The disappearance of *Developing Stories* from the schedules is not an isolated phenomenon. In the last five years, broadcast hours of documentary programmes on international issues have fallen by 40 per cent on UK television while in-depth views of life in the developing world have all but disappeared from popular mainstream peak-time slots. (Cleasby, A (1995) *What in the World is Going On? British Television and Global Affairs* 3WE.)

The less people see of the world the less they want to see and the more life elsewhere feels like a distant irrelevance, or even a threat, to them. Whatever the advances in news gathering technology, the loss of these contextualising programmes is having a disastrous effect on public awareness of the underlying issues – and the *humanity* – that make the world's newsworthy events significant in the first place.

Whether causal or coincidental, it would be hard to deny that there are links between parochial trends in broadcasting and rising xenophobia in society. In 1994, in the wake of a new Asylum Act, Britain granted refugee status to half the number of asylum seekers than in the previous year – just 824 out of 33,000 people claiming a well-founded fear of persecution. Changing the ground rules about what counts as 'well-founded' in order to restrict the number of incoming refugees is a pattern being repeated throughout Europe and beyond.

Global Dislocation

The insularising impact of demand-dominated, free-market forces on UK television may be typical of other industrialised nations but for many Southern countries the experience has been exactly the opposite.

Faustin Misanvu, Director of Ugandan Television has described the wide-reaching effects of the IMF's Structural Adjustment Programme on the national television network in Uganda (Misanvu, F (1994) from an informal address to the One World Broadcasting Trust Conference, London). Ugandan Television's stated policy is to achieve a 60:40 balance between locally produced programmes and imports but since the 'marketplace' has been 'opened up' according to the IMF's edicts, newly licensed broadcasters show virtually nothing but Northern imports like CNN, *The Oprah Winfrey Show* and bulk-buy titles from the catalogues of distributors like Warner Bros. Price is a determining factor here; a single edition of *Oprah* costs around US$100 while overheads for domestic production – training, cameras, editing equipment, staff costs, studios and so on – make home-grown programmes much more expensive.

The imports have their place but with no local news, local productions or local participation, the social and developmental benefits of this kind of unregulated, saturation broadcasting are difficult to imagine. In the over-zealous free-market economy, however, profit is the only measure of value so the Ugandan public service broadcaster is under pressure to cut costs. This experience is being repeated throughout Africa, South East Asia, Eastern Europe and Latin America.

Déjà Vu?

Some people in Northern countries – though depressingly few of us, it ought to be said – take the view that 19th century colonial missionaries often imposed alien cultural values on indigenous populations. Even though we appreciate how resilient such indigenous cultures can be, how adept they are at *appropriating* external influences for their own purposes, we are repulsed by the racist and culturally *inappropriate* behaviour of the colonists. In part I suppose we think like this because time has distanced us from the system of values and beliefs which condoned and promoted such evangelism.

The vast majority of people in the North remain too closely bound to the values and belief-structures of extractive capitalism to draw any parallels between the cultural coercion which occurred at the end of the 19th century and that taking place now, at the end of the 20th. The message may have changed from eternal salvation to 'Always Coca Cola'. The mode of communication might have shifted from sermons and soap boxes to soap operas and satellite dishes. But can anyone sensibly contend that cultural sensitivity has played a significant part in recent economic and developmental practices?

A Sense of Hope

In the 21st century we may be able to make such pluralistic claims. Democratisation of the media is upon us as technology becomes more affordable, miniaturised and user-friendly. Among many others, Sheldon Annis, senior research associate at the US Overseas Development Council, has noted the potency which increased use of the media

gives grassroots organisations. Pro-democracy groups in China are escaping the stranglehold of censorship by accessing information and activists around the globe through the Internet. The use of desktop publishing and video conferencing equipment in remote locations means indigenous groups like the Yanomami are able to share knowledge and coordinate plans in their battle for survival. Hi-8 cameras allow fishermen in Southern Honduras to supply video footage of the destruction of their mangroves to news organisations across the world and so increase popular pressure for political change in far-flung places.

This participation does not in itself eradicate poverty, end persecution or offer sanctuary to refugees but it does begin to weave the poor, the oppressed and the dispossessed into the civil fabric of our societies. This may alter radically the nature of that fabric and make positive change imperative and imminent.

Media Education

The development of our ability to communicate and interpret is where media education becomes crucial. Learning how to run a radio station, operate a video camera or work a computer terminal are relatively simple tasks. But critical pedagogy has its work cut out in helping us to learn the processes of constructing, perceiving, evaluating and reflecting on the significance of programmes, narratives, words and images.

A critical media education is the flipside of the coin of participatory media. Learning how the media works – how it represents reality and constructs meaning, how we read significance into its artefacts – empowers us to act on reconstructing it to serve the interests of democracy, social justice and sustainability. This can begin with primary school activities, continue with specialised secondary and adult learning and is increasingly a feature of the creative output of the media itself.

Watch the television films and educational video that are part of *The Right to Hope*, for example, and you will hear and see Joseph Madisia describing the importance of visual images in developing children's ability to understand and recall stories. Though we tend to think of media studies as a sophisticated activity suitable mainly for older students who are capable of analysing the nature of meaning, the structure of a narrative and so on, many primary school teachers are using television to help develop the basic literacy skills of very young children.

To get a clearer view of why we think literacy is so important, of what we are doing when we read, write and communicate, it may be useful to attend to the notion of what counts as text. The word stems from the Latin *textare*, 'to weave', and it shares this common root with 'textile'. There is a powerful and ancient Mesopotamian myth that civilisation only began when the first texts were created on the loom. We literally 'weave meaning into' the things we see and make. Likewise *texture* is not just the distinctive way a surface feels to the touch but also a verb which signifies the act of imbuing the surface with that distinctive feel. The importance of *context* – the before and after and surrounding details – in fleshing out and making comprehensive our understanding of anything has already been touched upon.

Examining how 'TV-texts' are selected and used in the classroom would probably throw up enough material for a whole new book. But it may be instructive to note that media-based education packs produced by organisations like Oxfam, Christian Aid and WWF-UK, or the educational output of production companies like the International Broadcasting Trust (IBT), Television Trust for the Environment (TVE) and the One World Group of Broadcasters often struggle to reach anything like a broad schools audience, let alone a mainstream adult viewership. These packs and

programmes are specifically created in cooperation with Southern partners to address, in a lively and participatory way, issues like sustainability, social justice, human rights and cross-cultural understanding.

A Sense of Responsibility

If we sincerely want to empower the voiceless people of our world and to enhance all our powers through the democratic, inclusive and sustainable processes of participatory media, we need to invest heavily, appropriately and soon in infrastructure and education. The Internet will only promote democracy if everyone can gain access to a computer; a modem is useless without a reliable telephone network; an illiterate population is much more likely to gorge itself on mindless entertainment than to seek empowerment and wisdom from its media.

The advent of participatory media is a rising tidal river running towards an ocean. So far the ocean's swell has successfully stemmed the flow, with commercial media organisations regarding our channels of communication merely as conduits to global markets ripe for exploitation. The vested interests of despotic governments and big businesses continue to dam democracy and sustainability. We can play a part in the Global Media Debate by prodding the consciences of the moguls who own the media machines, the legislators who govern them, the broadcasters who run them and the businesses who advertise through them. If we do this while all the time sharpening our own critical faculties then, like a rainy season in the uplands, we can make the river's progress unstoppable.

The whirlpools and eddies where the opposing flows meet can make the bigger picture difficult to grasp but part of our responsibility as practitioners and proponents of pluralism, peace and democracy is to keep the media constantly alive to that bigger picture. A parochial media reinforces the grip of xenophobia and racism in society and a glut of escapist trivia can breed a desperate fatalism. Many of us are no longer willing, it seems, to be treated *en masse* as undiscriminating, docile consumers. We are beginning to raise our voices, to film, watch and listen with care and to ask some difficult questions.

A Sense of Purpose

At the very beginning of this chapter, I mentioned one of those questions. I suggested it was deeply rooted, vexed and essentially ethical – then sheepishly refrained from attempting to phrase it. I have sought to imply that the media acts like a powerful undercurrent in our lives, which is why the question around which I have dallied is deeply rooted. I believe we must continually and relentlessly ask the question of ourselves and of our media providers, though the absence of a simple answer may cause many vexations. And its ethical essence lies in the continuing difficulty of choosing a path between the conflicting motivations of demand and need, profit and worth.

I think the question might usefully be put like this: 'What is the purpose of the media?' I do not mean to suggest that there is some point to mass communication in the sense of an end it is meant to achieve or a task it is designed to accomplish. There is another sense of 'purpose' which we use every day – 'how do the parts relate to the whole?' The purpose of our pupils is in seeing, though we are free to close our eyes. The purpose of a handle is in opening the door, though we can always choose to slam it shut.

When it comes to the media, this may seem like an insuperable question with which to leave you. The parts look like a chaotic jumble but I have tried to show that patterns do emerge when you take a number of viewpoints into account. Some of them are, at least potentially, liberating while others are cloying, isolating and disenfranchising. The whole is likewise far from being insuperable. It is, for each of us and all of us – in our individual autonomy, in our discreet and unique cultural groups and in our transcendant humanity – what we are and what we hope to become.

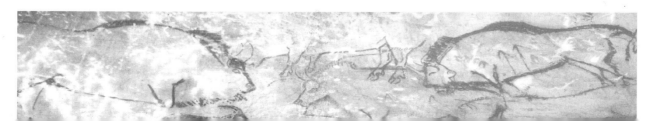

5

Population and Empowerment

Nafis Sadik

If humanity is to successfully confront the daunting social and development challenges it faces today, all individuals, women and men, must be empowered to make full use of their creative energies. Fortunately, the global community is becoming increasingly aware of the enormous power that would be unleashed if all peoples were enabled to participate in every aspect of development, as equals.

There is an emerging international consensus that the future depends on meeting human needs – notably, alleviating poverty, providing access to health care and education, and ensuring employment opportunities. Curbing wasteful consumption and production practices and bringing population into balance with natural resources are part of this effort. This vision focuses on empowering women and men, families, communities and nations to take charge of their destinies.

This consensus has taken shape over the course of a series of United Nations conferences, including the United Nations Conference on Environment and Development (Rio, 1992), the World Conference on Human Rights (Vienna, 1993), the International Conference on Population and Development (Cairo, 1994) and the World Summit for Social Development, held in Copenhagen in March 1995. It is likely to be developed further at the Fourth World Conference on Women in Beijing in September 1995 and the Habitat II Conference in Istanbul in 1996.

Common to these conferences is a call for social development which expands opportunities for individual women and men and their families, empowering them to attain their social, economic, political and cultural aspirations. Only through such a human development perspective can truly sustainable development be achieved.

The International Conference on Population and Development (ICPD), in particular, was notable for its emphasis on gender equity, equality and the empowerment of women both as important ends in themselves and as necessary to the attainment of sustainable development. A central focus was on reproductive and sexual health as fundamental human rights. The conference in Cairo, where I served as Secretary-General, adopted a set of 20-year goals including reduction of maternal, infant and child mortality, with particular emphasis on eliminating gender disparities; increased access to education, especially for girls; and universal access to a broad range of quality reproductive health care and family planning services.

Raising people's awareness and helping to change outdated attitudes are critical to fulfilling these goals. As *The Right to Hope* project so vividly shows, art and culture can play a powerful role in this regard.

Background

The world today has nearly 5.7 billion people. More than one billion live in absolute poverty, and many more are only marginally better off. Infant, child and maternal mortality rates are still tragically high in many countries despite

the substantial progress achieved in recent decades. Throughout the world, women and girls face tremendous disadvantages with regard to health care, education, training and employment prospects.

Globally, basic resources on which future generations will depend are being depleted. There is a vicious cycle of poverty, social and economic inequality, rapid population growth, environmental degradation, and unsustainable production and consumption patterns. Uncontrolled urban growth and a steady increase in international migration are among the consequences.

In the past thirty years, developing countries have made significant gains in providing better and more comprehensive primary health care, including reproductive health care and family planning. The result has been lower birth and death rates, increased life expectancy and reduced infant mortality. This progress is linked to higher levels of education and income, a narrowing 'gender gap' in health and education, increased political commitment to population policies, and changes in individual attitudes about family planning. Contraceptive use has increased dramatically in recent years.

These achievements, however, have been uneven. Infant, child and maternal mortality rates are still tragically high in many developing countries despite the substantial progress achieved in recent decades. Maternal death rates are 15–50 times greater in the developing world than in most developed countries. Half a million women still die each year as a consequence of pregnancy and childbirth. Nearly all of these deaths are in developing countries; most could be prevented with quality pre-natal examinations, proper medical referrals and emergency obstetric care. For each maternal death, many more women – a much larger number than was previously thought – suffer from illness or impairment related to pregnancy and childbirth.

While levels of education have risen and the gap between males and females has narrowed, there are still nearly 960 million illiterate persons in the world, two-thirds of them women; some 130 million children, including over 90 million girls, are denied access to primary schooling.

Women have been entering the labour force in record numbers, many of them in non-traditional economic roles. But women are often the principal or only source of support for themselves and their children. And women still have less access than men to training, credit, property, natural resources and better-paid jobs.

The ongoing shift of rural populations to urban areas is placing increasing strains on the resources of developing countries. At the same time, migration between countries continues to rise. In many countries, longer life expectancy and declining birth rates are increasing the proportion of elderly people in the population.

Access to family planning, contraceptive use, and the average family size vary widely among countries and regions. Worldwide, some 350 million couples lack access to a full range of modern family planning information and services; an estimated 120 million women would practise family planning if a modern method were available, affordable and acceptable to their partners, families and communities. Enabling all couples and individuals to exercise their right to determine the size of their families, and whether and when to have children, is a vital aspect of empowering women and giving them more choices in life.

Women in most societies cannot participate fully in economic and public life, have limited access to positions of influence and power, have narrower occupational choices and lower earnings than men, and must struggle to reconcile activities outside the home with their traditional roles. Too often, they have little or no voice in decisions made in or outside the household. These inequities must be redressed to fulfil women's human rights and enable countries to progress towards sustainable development.

Together with health care, education is the most important issue in breaking the vicious cycle of low status, poverty and large families. There is a direct connection between education for girls and women's ability to escape from poverty;

education also encourages later marriage and greater use of contraception. It is associated with lower maternal mortality, with smaller, healthier families; and better reproductive health for the next generation.

While girls have edged nearer to parity with boys in primary school enrolment in much of the world, parents still tend to give preference to educating their sons. In most countries, the higher the level of education, the lower the proportion of women to men. Numerous innovative programmes are helping to increase and sustain female educational achievement; these need to be maintained and expanded.

While health issues related to reproduction and sexuality affect women and men of all ages, women bear most of the associated burden of ill health.

A New Approach

The ICPD approach recognises that to improve people's quality of life and health, developing countries must have sustained economic growth within a framework of sustainable development; they must invest in health and education, especially for girls; and women must be empowered so that their social, political, economic and health status matches that of men.

The ICPD was the successor to the World Population Conference held in Bucharest in 1974 and the International Conference on Population held in Mexico City in 1984. Agreements reached at those gatherings contributed greatly to the enormous progress that developing countries have made over the past 20 years in expanding access to family planning and in addressing other population issues.

In preparing for the 1994 conference, however, a distinctly new approach evolved. This new strategy grew out of the experience of the two previous decades, and the global community's growing appreciation of the importance of human development, environmental protection and the empowerment of women. It emphasises the many links between population and development, and focuses on meeting the needs of individual women and men rather than on achieving demographic targets. Non-governmental organisations (NGOs), particularly women's groups, played an unprecedented role in shaping the ICPD Programme of Action. The approach adopted in Cairo has several key premises:

- **First,** efforts to slow population growth, alleviate poverty, achieve economic progress, improve environmental protection, and reduce unsustainable consumption and production are so closely linked that none can succeed in isolation. Consequently, all planning for sustainable development needs to take into account demographic factors such as population growth and distribution, age structure, mortality, fertility and migration.

- **Second,** investing in people, in their health and education, is the key to sustained economic growth and sustainable development.

- **Third,** there can be no sustainable development without the full and equal participation of women in all aspects of development planning and programming.

- **Fourth,** care for a full range of reproductive health concerns should be made universally available through primary health care systems as part of a comprehensive strategy that includes, among others: pre-natal care, safe delivery, post-natal care, family planning, reproductive tract infections, sexually transmitted diseases including HIV/AIDS, infertility, and prevention of abortion and management of the complications of abortion.

- **Fifth,** a holistic approach to population policy which starts with concern for the individual would result in reduced population growth rates and stabilisation of world population at a much lower level than that which would result from the top-down approach based on demographic goals.

Other components of the ICPD consensus include: a commitment to end all forms of violence against women, including harmful practices like female genital mutilation; an agreement on the need to provide adolescents with appropriate information and services in regard to sexuality and reproductive health; and a recognition that men need to take responsibility for their sexual and reproductive behaviour and share family and household responsibilities equally with women.

Results

Throughout the world, one can find many examples of programmes that embody the ICPD approach of striving to increase the choices available to people, especially women:

- In the Philippine province of Capiz, a project to raise the incomes and status of disadvantaged women has provided loans and technical assistance, allowing women's groups to start small businesses to cultivate and sell seafood. As a result, a number of poor fishing villages now have improved health care, family planning and better resource management.
- The Working Women's Forum, based in Madras, India, has brought income-generation and family welfare opportunities to an estimated 150,000 urban and rural families. The project offers night classes for working children, loans for businesswomen, and health services which have nearly doubled family planning use and child immunisation since 1980.
- The NGO Tanzania Legal Scheme for Women runs workshops to inform women of their rights, provides free legal representation to women who assert their property rights in court, and urges women to run for political office.
- 'Partners in Population and Development: A South-South Initiative', launched last year by ten nations, is enabling developing countries to become more self-reliant in reproductive health care and family planning by sharing experiences, training programmes, technical know-how and locally manufactured contraceptive supplies.
- In Ghana, where the average woman still has more than five children, funding to establish clinics and train staff in providing family planning and obstetric care has helped, over a four-year period, to improve reproductive health significantly and to double the percentage of couples using modern contraception.
- The Jamaica Women's Centre aims to free young women from the cycle of marginalisation and repeated pregnancy through education and counselling. Young mothers are encouraged to return to school after giving birth; their newborns can stay in the nursery at the centre while they are in class. Fathers are also encouraged to be involved in the programme, and many attend the weekly community workshops.

Political and Financial Commitment Needed

Successful implementation of the ICPD Programme of Action will require both political commitment and substantial financial resources. The Cairo conference estimated that a comprehensive package of reproductive health care and family

planning services for developing countries and those with economies in transition would cost $17 billion per year in the year 2000 and $21.7 billion in 2015. It is anticipated that the countries themselves will be able to provide two-thirds of the necessary funds. About one-third, amounting to $5.7 billion in 2000 and $7.2 billion in 2015, will have to come from donors.

The agreement in Cairo on the need for this level of international support was in itself a ringing endorsement of the practical value of the ICPD Programme. Since the conference, a number of countries have already indicated that they will increase their support for population programmes.

Another key ingredient of successful implementation will be the full involvement of non-governmental organisations in formulating, executing, monitoring and evaluating population and development-related programmes. The Programme of Action recognises this and explicitly calls for effective partnership between governments and NGOs.

The Programme of Action opens the way for increased cooperation among countries to reach their common goals. At the same time, nothing in the ICPD consensus weakens the power of nations to make their own decisions regarding population and development. Chapter II emphasises that implementation is:

> *the sovereign right of each country, consistent with national laws and development priorities, with full respect for the various religious and ethical values and cultural backgrounds of its people, and in conformity with universally recognised international human rights.*

An Essential Blueprint

While ICPD was a tremendous success, our work did not end in Cairo; rather, the conference marked the beginning of a new phase in dealing with the immense challenges of population and development. And the ICPD Programme of Action provides an essential blueprint for facing those challenges in the next twenty years.

Implementing this holistic approach, based on the principle of free, informed choice, will have the effect of promoting smaller, healthier families. Lower birth rates will lead to a better balance between population growth and resources. The ICPD demonstrated the advantages of action, and the cost of failure. Energetic and committed implementation of the Programme of Action over the next twenty years will bring women into the mainstream of development; protect their health, promote their education, and encourage and reward their economic contribution; ensure that every pregnancy is intended, and every child a wanted child; protect women from the results of unsafe abortion; protect the health of adolescents, and encourage responsible behaviour; combat HIV/AIDS; promote education for all and close the gender gap in education; and protect and promote the integrity of the family.

The Programme of Action will as a result contribute to slower and more balanced population growth; to the ending of poverty; and to economic development compatible with the demands of sustainability.

This programme of education and health care will empower every individual, thereby nurturing human initiative and creativity and giving us all, women, men and children, the right to hope for a peaceful and sustainable future.

6

SATYAGRAHA

Anil Agarwal

When I look back at the last 23 years of my career as an environmental journalist, beginning with the mega Stockholm Conference in 1972, I find I have changed little. From the start of my journalistic career, I have remained deeply pessimistic about the immediate future but equally deeply optimistic about the long term.

It was Barbara Ward, founder of the International Institute for Environment and Development, where I worked for three long years in the late 1970s, who said that everyone has the 'right to hope'. I cannot agree more with her because the social injustice and economic disparity that stares millions of poor people in the face, even as we move into the 21st century, leaving behind an otherwise highly productive century for humankind in almost all walks of life, would make life impossible without that 'right to hope'. As long as the world sticks largely to democratic systems of governance, I am convinced that one day the poor will get better organised and the rich will have the sagacity enough to see their betterment in the empowerment and enrichment of those worse off than themselves.

As a young engineer in training during the late 1960s, I grew up to witness an India facing a serious economic and food crisis arising out of consecutive and severe droughts, and heavily dependent on food aid. Its economy in shambles and the main political party, the Indian National Congress, beginning to crack for the first time, the national honour was shamed repeatedly by a defeat at the hands of the Chinese in 1962 and an unsure victory over the Pakistanis in 1965; and a nationwide Maoist rebellion emerging in various parts of the country. The prestigious engineering education we received did not seem to provide any answers to the economic situation governing the half-a-million odd villages, many of which surrounded literally the very institute where we were getting educated. And indeed, nor were many of my colleagues interested in this challenge. They were the brightest minds in India, but they were happy to migrate and meet the simpler challenges of the industrialised world to earn their living.

For some of us, quite contrary to what most of us thought, Mahatma Gandhi, the long-forgotten Father of the independent nation called India, and the permanent revolutionary, Mao Tse Tung of China, who at that time had embroiled his nation in a high-minded Cultural Revolution, had some answers to the problem of the poor and their poverty. Both Gandhi and Mao had talked of small technology, of 'not mass production but production by the masses', of empowerment and control as some of the answers to the problem of economic growth among the poor. Gandhi had seen how colonialism had destroyed an entire nation within a span of two to three centuries, from a nation that was one of the richest, most urbanised and most literate to a nation that was one of the poorest, least urbanised and the most illiterate – by a power whose monarchy at one time did not even have the wealth of the pettiest of petty Indian nobles or lords. Even today, the Queen of that nation proudly displays a precious stone in her crown which was stolen from this country.

Gandhi had also seen the country change dramatically during those ill-forsaken years. The cities that today dominate the Indian economy – Bombay, Calcutta and Madras – did not even exist in the pre-colonial days. India's urban economy was organised in totally different ways and deeply integrated with its hinterland. But by the time

independence came to India, Gandhi's call to his country to turn its back on the creations of the coloniser and look once again for its fountain of growth in its poor and its villages – the last man, as he puts it – was by then too backward-looking a philosophy even for his fellow politicians.

During the 1950s and early 1960s, the euphoria of independence, of industrialisation, of the opportunity to catch up with the West, had caught the nation's elite and its imagination. I was one of the few hundreds, selected out of a competitive exam in which nearly half a million had tried, who were going to build that new nation. But by the late 1980s, that great dream was cracking. The Swedish economist Gunnar Myrdal was once again remembering the value of The Mahatma in his magnum opus, *The Asian Drama*. And as someone was to put it later, India was beginning to discover that there was no grass at its roots.

It was with this frame of mind that I went to report on my first major conference as a young journalist. The Stockholm Conference brought together thousands of activists, thinkers and politicians. Activists like those from *The Ecologist* group wanted to save the world with their *Blueprint for Survival* but few of them cared to ask: Save the world for whom? The filthy rich of the North and equally filthy rich of the South or for the poor millions of the world? In the background of everyone's consciousness was the Meadows' report, *Limits to Growth*, which was all very well after everything was said and done; but even to a young engineer like me, familiar with number crunching exercises, the model was a bit too simplistic. But there were many other moving experiences too at Stockholm. I sat spellbound listening to Barbara Ward tell the delegates in one of the most powerful speeches I have ever heard that 150-odd nations cannot divide and decide upon a world that is essentially one. Her book, *Only One Earth*, spelt out the very spirit of the Conference. But even as Barbara was trying to bring the world together, Sweden's great Prime Minister, Olaf Palme, was reminding the world of the stark reality of power and powerlessness. He said in no uncertain terms that the Conference was somewhat of a farce when one member-nation of the international community, the United States, was deliberately destroying the environment of another nation, Vietnam. And, of course, our own Prime Minister, the late Mrs Indira Gandhi, worried that the environment could be used as an excuse to slow down the economic growth of developing nations, pointed out to the Conference, in an oft-quoted statement, 'poverty is the biggest polluter'. In other words, unless countries like India got rid of their poverty, they could not save the environment. In between all the razzmatazz, I stole time to nail down my favourite author, Gunnar Myrdal, to ask him, 'What impact do you think your books are having or will have? Is there anyone out there listening to your advice?' 'I write what I think is right,' the great thinker replied. 'Books are like time bombs. If what I have written is wrong, history will forget me. But if what I have written is right, then one day the ideas in those books will definitely explode.' I have never forgotten that answer as a writer and author myself. So close indeed, I now realise, to the key thought in the great Hindu text, the Gita: You do your duty because it is only on your duty that you have a right. Don't worry about the fruits. The Gita also tells you that the fruits of your actions are inevitable. But when and how you will reap those fruits should not be a matter of worry to you.

I went from Stockholm to London and sought out an old economist, E F Schumacher, who was at that time writing a fascinating book. We met in a noisy pub in Charing Cross station, and he excitedly told me about his forthcoming book, *Small is Beautiful*, which was to take the world by storm with the idea of intermediate technology or as it was later rechristened, appropriate technology, in order to deal with the reactionary onslaught of the big technology gang. However, I could not share Schumacher's enthusiasm and repeatedly asked him: 'So what is new about your ideas?' Finally, the sweet old man lost his cool and said sharply: 'Yes, of course, for a person coming from the land of Gandhi, nothing! But for Westerners, a lot.'

To that, I agreed completely. Here was a man, I thought, who was going to translate Gandhian thinking so brilliantly, when it no longer existed in his own country. But I could not fail to see that Schumacher had not thought through the politics of his thought in the modern, late 20th century world. I was not sure if his thoughts would bring about much change.

I returned to India very confused about the environmental issue. What was the relevance of environmental concern to India? What was the relevance to my own city, Kanpur, which under the British was one of the country's leading industrial cities, but had now deteriorated into a sprawling, dirty, filthy, absolutely obnoxious slum, literally a hell-hole for humanity? I was convinced that India needed economic growth and investments, without which the poor would never find the jobs and the investments needed to keep the city and its air and water clean. Western environmentalists, it seemed to me, were only worried about the survival of their own societies. As the editor of *Nature*, John Maddox, was to tell me in a critical interview in New Delhi, 'They have all the wealth. Now they also want clean air and clean water. How can such a concern be of interest to the developing world?'

Yet I was deeply impressed by a short, three-day stay in a youth hostel in Oslo. The nation was geared up to a referendum on whether it should join the European Economic Commission or not. I met people in hostels, in colleges and in parks. And everyone was so animated about it: No, we will not join. There were, of course, many, many considerations. But one of them definitely was: We will not let those Germans and others come and spoil our environment. Having seen what *laissez faire* over the last 200 years had done to the environment of my country under which the coloniser could do whatever it wanted, I sympathised with the fear of the Norwegians. But most of all, I saw democracy at work. A nation in which everyone's opinion mattered.

Fortunately, within a matter of two years, my confusion was going to disappear. As a young reporter for the *Hindustan Times*, working under an extremely sensitive and development-minded editor, B G Verghese, I was approached by a sincere and committed expert on Himalayan flora, Virendra Kumar, about a story that had deeply touched him. He was trying to set up a laboratory deep in the Himalayas, especially in the unique Valley of Flowers, with the help of fertiliser bags, Buckminster Fuller-type bamboo domes and wooden micro-hydel units to power his equipment. He had come across a movement in which women had threatened to hug the trees and would not let them be cut by the state-sponsored contractor. He had now been asked by the state's chief minister to chair a committee to decide whether the women, or the experts of the forest department, were right about the environmental consequences of the state's decision to auction the forest. Strangely, the events he was describing were more than a year old but nobody had heard about them or written about them in the powerful English media in New Delhi, where I served. Armed with the permission of the editor, I trekked up to the remote forest which was to be cut, met the women who had made that enigmatic threat, and, of course, various activists who all claimed their role in the struggle. I came back a changed person.

It was a great story – possibly the greatest of my life. Considering that the event that was so old and, moreover, an environment story, I made the second lead of the leading national daily. And the editor gave me the best 'story of the month' award. But the Chipko (tree hugging) movement changed me far more deeply. No longer would I ever believe a brown or a white man telling me – in fact, I would throw hammers at such people in later years – that the poor cannot care for their environment. On the contrary, I have since lived with the abiding belief that it is the educated and the rich who are the most environment-illiterate. I also realised that dear Mrs Gandhi, as with many educated Indians like me, knew precious little about her own country and her own people. A concerned environmentalist undoubtedly, but like all rich people worldwide, her responses were still in a conservationist mould. So too was the West, caught up

in the travails of pollution, of the threat of Silent Springs and widespread nuclear radiation.

But the poor were speaking with an utilitarian ethic, not a conservationist ethic. Gandhi and Chipko were talking about using the environment but in a manner that was socially just and non-destructive. The environment slowly got transformed for me into the natural resource base and, in the case of the poor, literally their survival base. Throughout the 1970s, I would tick off people ranting and raving about the excess numbers of people in the world, about the way the poor destroyed forests for their firewood, about the way the forests were disappearing and the land was being destroyed in poor countries. Working at the International Institute for Environment and Development, I found the West, on the one hand, deeply democratic and transparent, but on the other hand (and overall), extremely arrogant, selfish and unabashedly stupid and ignorant about the 'rest of the world'. Gandhi and Chipko had given me a very Indian third eye to observe the West and I repeatedly saw it lacking in understanding of 'the other'.

Yet what touched me most in the West was its own democracy. That debates could be conducted in a society without fear. That television commentators could ask rude and difficult questions even to their Prime Ministers. That so many young people could collectively challenge the capitalist invaders regarding the environmental consequences of their actions. The environmental movement was, in fact, redefining the very terms of democracy in the West. Built upon the principles of representative democracy, Western democracy gave people the right to elect their leaders but then gave their leaders, till they were thrown out, considerable rights to decide the future of the people. The growing environmental movement of the young was, however, not impressed. It was telling the likes of Callaghan and Thatcher that they did not have untrammelled power simply because they were Prime Minister. If their decisions invaded people's habitats, the people had a right to protest and say 'no'. This was derisively called the 'Not in my Back Yard'(NIMBY) philosophy. But this philosophy was making representative democracy more participatory and strengthening local democracy. A new post-war generation was beginning to assert itself. And where local democracy was stronger, within the nations of the West itself, the environmental movement had a greater and deeper impact. While the ex-imperial nations like France and the United Kingdom lagged behind, the Swiss, the Dutch and the Scandinavians took a lead.

Back in India, too, there was a lot more to learn. There was lots more that my generation was learning from Chipko. That in their relationship to their natural resources, men and women, conditioned by their respective roles determined by a male-dominated culture, responded differently to their environment. That the local community constituted – more than any other economic agent, the state bureaucracy or the private entrepreneur, for instance – the best economic agent from the point of view of sustainability and of sustainable use of natural resources: it had, in fact, the greatest vested interest in sustainability that could be found in any economic agent.

Worldwide, however, there was still considerable confusion. In conference after conference, people would still argue that development must take precedence over environment in the poor, developing nations of the world. Environmental concerns were still seen as a luxury in the face of gruelling poverty and massive unemployment. The general attitude was that they could wait. In 1982, working together with several other concerned people and the small group of people called environmentalists at that time, the Centre for Science and Environment in New Delhi produced a citizens' report on the state of India's environment. The report did not just document the trends in environmental degradation but also how this degradation was affecting the lives of its people. It was the first such report of its kind in the world. And it showed in dramatic detail how the poor, living and subsisting on the margins of the environment, are the ones who suffer the most when the environment degrades. In a poor, biomass-subsistence economy which also has a high population density, the report showed that the people had occupied nearly every environmental space for their survival. The rivers and lakes were full of poor fisherfolk, the grasslands full of nomadic shepherds and buffalo herders, even the irrigated rice fields were full of duck herders, and, of course, the forests were full of forest-dwelling people.

Every time this environment was destroyed by a process of development, there were always people who bore the brunt of that destruction. Thus, every act against nature in a country like India clearly was an act against humanity itself. It increased impoverishment and by destroying the survival base, it increased even unemployment, and no act of development could, therefore, be even called development, by its very own definition, unless it was environmentally sound. Environmental destruction and social injustice became, thus, two sides of the same coin.

This documentation helped to clear many cobwebs in our minds. It confirmed the attitude that poor nations could wait to take care of their environment while the steamroller of development could go along its path of destruction. As the 1980s went by, several new dimensions of the link between poverty and environment began to emerge. Now that we no longer saw just the physical aspects of the environment, but more people living in the environment, it was only a small step forward to appreciate the role of popular culture in governing the human interactions of the people. Their ways of doing things, their traditional techniques, their history and beliefs and their knowledge about their surrounding plant and animal world, their history of natural resource use and of ecological change – all increasingly began to look important.

For me – and I am sure for a lot of environmentalists – who never learnt any of this in school, this has been a long, long educational process, and it has taken us to the very roots of our societies. We have emerged from this journey with ever-increasing pride and with a deep sense of prejudice towards the dynamism and innovativeness of the poor. Judge them by whatever standards and they emerge as good as any. In numerous lectures on biodiversity, I have asked people the question: 'Who can you think of as the greatest economic contributor to the world, whose contributions have touched nearly every human being's life?' Few people give the correct answer. Surely not Ford. How many people drive cars? Surely not IBM. How many people even today use computers? No, not even that dear old man, Albert Einstein. No, in fact, no white man by even a mile. You will be surprised: the American Indians gave this world corn, chocolate, potato, tomato, rubber and quinine, to name just a few. Just think of the numbers who have benefited from quinine. Just think how many have eaten corn and just think of how many have eaten potatoes. Probably just about everyone. In terms of economic contributors, the Fords and the Rockefellers are, in comparison, not even equal to good shoeshine boys. But where in the world have you heard that before – or worse, why were you never taught that in school, made to write it down 1000 times on the blackboard so that you would never forget it in your entire lifetime? So that the educated like you and me would keep their arrogance in check.

This is all but a summary of an evolution of ideas over two decades. Action in the environmental field has not been stagnant either. Ideas have developed from the action and vice versa. As the understanding of environmental issues has grown, many communities and NGOs have taken action to protect and use their environment rationally. Their efforts have been supported by the growing NGO sector. The three great strengths of Indian NGOs have been in:

1. *creating environmental awareness and raising public consciousness of the environmental challenges ahead;*
2. *firefighting against environmentally destructive projects; and*
3. *developing new, innovative and participatory models of natural resource management.*

It is in the last area that Indian NGOs have truly excelled. In forest management, in water management and in numerous other areas, NGOs have worked closely with local communities to take control of their destiny by taking control of their environment and developing resource management regimes that are equitable and participatory. The work of Chandi Prasad Bhatt in the Chamoli district, of Priya Ratna Mishra in Sukhomajri village and in the Palamu

district, of Vilas Salunke in the formation of Pani Panchayats in rural Pune, and of Anna Hazare in Ralegan Siddhi are all outstanding and pioneering examples of how the poor can generate sustainable wealth through the regeneration of their environment. And there are many more such experiments which have followed.

The question that has intrigued me is, why did all these disconnected and disparate efforts emerge in different parts of India in the mid- to late 1970s? Several of them had no external agent except an inspired leader at the village level. Very few of these people – from Salunke to Mishra – were environmentalists in the modern sense of the word. The environmental movement has adopted them as environmentalists, but they did what they had to do because of their local compulsions and not just environmental concerns. Yet all of them made the establishment of a good natural resource management regime their key objective with equity and participation as its two key elements.

Increasingly I am convinced that what we are witnessing is a societal response to an emerging ecological and associated social and economic crisis. The crisis is not very old. Access to natural resources has declined sharply only in a few decades. On the one hand, there has been the impact of uncontrolled development leading to rapid degradation of the resource base. And on the other, there has been this relentless population growth. In just 30 years, between 1950 and 1980, India's population doubled. Never before had the country's population doubled with such speed. Over a few decades, whatever resources people had effectively shrunk by half. And if there was also a process of degradation going on because of development, they shrank probably to one-tenth and in some cases to nothing. Surely neither the people nor their movers and shakers like the Bhatts, Mishras and Hazares could remain mute witnesses to a slow erosion of their very survival base. A time had come when the people had to respond. And I think there is enough evidence to show that they are beginning to respond now. The Chipko protests took place in the early 1970s. But in the 1980s what was even more heartening was the attempt of thousands of villages in south Bihar, in West Bengal and in Orissa to protect and regenerate their forests even though they are still legally owned by the state. How much, indeed, do social scientists know about the way poor people see the changing world and what they are planning to do about it? The answer is, given all their biases, especially their bias towards projects and tarmac, social scientists know precious little. More correctly, precisely nothing. But the more I travel, I see Chipko not as an aberration but a daily reality. Chipko was a very beautiful and a very enigmatic, non-violent statement of protest. Fortunately, it came to and caught the attention of the world. But few such protests get the same coverage or attention. This is not because they do not exist, but because they are the reality of a powerless majority.

What is lagging behind in this change today is not people's action but the system of governance – a system left behind by the colonisers and adopted by the post-independence elite to perpetuate its own control. The worst enemies of the poor today are the bureaucrats and the professionals who deny them everything. Firstly, they deny them any knowledge, wisdom and, therefore, any self-respect; and secondly, they refuse to let them have any control over the management of their resource base. The worst enemies of the poor are the professionals. I cannot think of a better statement against the professionals than Ivan Illich's *Disabling Professions*. I am absolutely convinced that it is the growth of professionalism, rather than the growth of capitalism, that has done the biggest damage to the world's poor. Often, even professional environmentalists play the same game of denying people the right to control the environment and placing greater trust in bureaucratic solutions. Today, this is the biggest challenge before the environmental movement of India and of the South in general: how can it translate the numerous, small village-level efforts to manage the environment into national strategies for nationwide rural renewal? This battle will inevitably be won. The educated professionals – the foresters, the irrigation engineers, the agricultural scientists, the economic planners and the service bureaucrats – are not going to give up control. But as the crisis grows, the transaction costs of bureaucratic management will inevitably grow and one day the

politician, facing elections, will have to take up the cudgel against the professional classes. This, I am convinced, will happen despite the media's fascination with the professionals and bureaucrats, because they are of the same ilk and are classed as journalists, as against the constant media criticism of politicians. It's not going to happen soon. But it *will* happen.

In many ways, a similar change is needed at the international level. But here I am not so optimistic. The 1980s saw several global environmental issues come to the fore and the answer to each one of them has been found in an international treaty – from ozone layer depletion to biodiversity conservation. Not in economic instruments or equal entitlements to the environment. Nor in globally valid judicial systems that can bring even the most powerful nations to book. Western environmental groups – from Greenpeace to Friends of the Earth – have all welcomed these treaties. They have, however, signally failed to study any of these treaties from the point of view of equity and social justice. The Montreal Protocol (treaty on the control of the use of ozone depleting substances) promoted by the likes of Ronald Reagan and Margaret Thatcher is absolutely the most dishonest and fraudulent environmental treaty ever thrust upon humanity and yet no green protest has ever been registered against it.

I am not surprised. The Western green movement can only try to achieve what its society will allow it to achieve. Western societies are today interested in saving the environment – for themselves and at as low a cost to their economy as possible. Western green groups respond to that felt need. But how these problems should be tackled on a global scale that is both fair and just is neither a high point on their own agenda nor on their society's agenda. Wolfgang Sachs, a leading German green thinker and chairperson of Greenpeace Germany, said at the time of the Berlin Summit on global warming that it was a conference to protect the national economy and not the global ecology. He was dead right. But when I asked, 'If that is the case and the explicit understanding of western NGOs, then why hasn't even one of them analysed with any iota of sincerity the products of these conferences – the various environmental treaties – that have emerged since the late 1980s?', his clear answer was: 'There is too much fascination with global things. If something is global it must be good.' Southern NGOs must get together to tell the Western Greens that not everything global is green. More often it reeks of dishonesty and corruption. The more we manage the world as one, the better it is. But this management must be fair, just and democratic. To put it bluntly, if there is a cost involved, the societies that have destroyed the most must pay the most. So what if there is going to be more poverty or unemployment? Ecological restructuring will demand as heavy a price as many developing nations have paid for squandering their economic resources in the 1970s and for the consequent economic restructuring they had to accept in the 1980s.

On this count, I am, however, least hopeful. I think the Southern Greens will be able to bring about a fundamental change in resource management over time, slowly but steadily. The people's pressure will give them the support they need. The change will be gradual but it will definitely take place. But in the North, I don't see this happening. The Greens do not have the backing of their societies – though, of course, there will be great differences in the responses of different Western nations – to demand fair and just changes on a global scale. Nor do I think they have the power of *satyagraha* (meaning, from Gandhi's philosophy, the power to assert the truth) to show how morally impoverished the actions of their societies are on a global scale. But, slowly, quietly, there are voices raising questions, voices calling for the truth; I can only assert my 'right to hope' and pray to God that my optimism about the future will be justified.

7

IDEALISM IN PRACTICE: COMPREHENDING THE INCOMPREHENSIBLE

Mary Midgley

My question is rather a strange one. How can we think about dilemmas which are manifestly too big for us to handle?

We are not actually the first people who have faced this problem, though we often feel as if we were. Earlier ages have been every bit as confusing and dangerous as ours for the people who lived in them. It may be true that our age is in fact even more confused and dangerous than any other era. But that claim makes very little difference for the people concerned. You can lose hope and drown just as well in seven feet of water as in seventy.

There have been, then, many desperately confused epochs everywhere. In Europe, for instance, the future seemed utterly hopeless for many people during the break-up of the Roman Empire and again during the early years of the Industrial Revolution. The reformers who then set about abolishing the slave trade, or attacking the state of the factories in the 1840s, or rewriting political theory (as Marx did) after the failed revolutions of 1848, needed a remarkable degree of courage to keep up their hope. But people did do these apparently irrational things. And, though their neighbours told them that it would be much more sensible to collapse into fatalistic inertia, we all probably think now that they were right to neglect that advice.

This leads back to my rather odd question. How can we attack the sort of problem they attacked? How can we confront dilemmas which are – as those other dilemmas were for the people of their day – manifestly too big for us even to conceive of properly, let alone to handle? It is as if we have to make our way through an unknown, confused and dangerous landscape. We need maps – that is, suitable ways of thinking. Those maps have to be limited and simplified enough to bring out the features that we need to see. Yet they must be detailed enough to make those features plain. They must be truthful enough to warn us about the difficulties, but they must not be so alarming that we get utterly discouraged.

Our maps – our ways of thinking – must be selective, but that does not make them misleading. The people who have managed to retrieve desperate situations in the past have done so by somehow making themselves maps of this kind. They have formed ideas that brought out the central issues, making them look clear and limited enough to tackle. They have managed to envisage crucial possibilities that have not yet been considered. This effort saved the people of their time from being paralysed by the mere tangle of conflicting considerations. Of course it did not provide ready-made solutions, but it made the search for solutions possible.

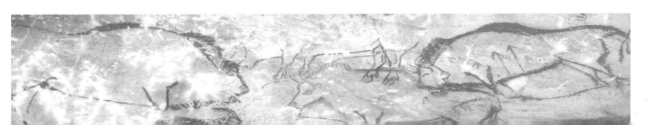

Defences against Thought

The interesting point is that, in these crises, it is not – as people often suspect – practical to stop thinking altogether. During periods of drastic change, new ideas are not a luxury. They are needed both as a tool for action and as a help to preserving sanity – both so that we can envisage our problems effectively and in order to avoid psychic disaster. Producing these useful ideas is, however, not easy, which is why we often use instead some of the other, much less satisfactory defence mechanisms that are always at hand.

The simplest of these defences is, of course, simply to forget about large-scale troubles altogether. We must all do this sometimes, but if we do it too much it can have a heavy cost in psychic numbing and narrowing, even sometimes in depression and despair. Self-isolation blocks the springs of our life because it cuts us off from reality. Even for our own inner health, to get things in perspective, we need sometimes to turn our minds to these monstrous topics.

I think it is worthwhile to attend here to the psychology of confronting – or not confronting – these vast dilemmas. Of course this psychological problem is a small one compared with the dilemmas themselves. But the smaller problem concerns us so directly that it can be helpful to look at it on its own.

Our next simplest defence (then), after mere avoidance, is polarising the question before us. We see it as a feud, a simple, ritual combat between political tribes. We wage crusades or *jihads* on behalf of the tribe that we support, writing off our opponents as totally mistaken. Still more absurdly, we tend to think of these opponents as being wholly responsible for the current disaster.

This impulse to polarise – to personify the issues as a contest – is very strong and I don't think that we fully understand it. Some tribal loyalty of this kind does almost necessarily enter into our political efforts. By giving us strength it can, up to a point, be useful. But we need to be on the watch for its undesirable effects. Looking at any dispute in which we are not actually involved, we can usually see how this kind of crude confrontation distorts the issues. But it is surprisingly hard to remember this when we are personally involved.

Next, if we become disillusioned with the various campaigns that demand our support, we may fall into an even odder polarisation, one that sets thought itself against non-thought. On the one hand, we may claim to be anti-intellectual Realists, rejecting all argument as mere theory, irrelevant to practice. People's idealistic thoughts and intentions seem then to be just an idle fifth wheel in the world's mechanism, not affecting the outcome. Indeed, from this position, words like *Idealism* become simply terms of abuse. Or, on the other hand, we may sign up as Idealists who are too pure to dirty ourselves with practical action at all.

This game of Realist versus Idealist keeps us paralysed because it divides the two sides of our own nature, sides that need to work together for action. It divides them even if (as can happen) a mild case of it is combined with the crusading habit rather than replacing it. Thus, while conducting a crusade, we may choose to play the role of victims, Idealists who are misunderstood by the Realists. We then lose interest in the critical thinking that might bring these sides together. We refuse to think about practical difficulties, which means we cannot act or choose any positive policy for action. This can happen even to people who are officially clamouring for immediate change. It is one of the commonest paralysing factors that waste the goodwill available for reform.

If, on the other hand, we choose to play as a Realist who understands the facts but is bored by ideals, we may know what the possibilities are all right. But, having decided that the *status quo* cannot be changed, we shall never find any reason to use this knowledge (what is commonly known as the 'Civil Servant's Syndrome').

Divisions of Labour

It is surprisingly difficult to combine these two sides of our nature. One very common way of doing it is to take them in sequence, to start life as an Idealist and become a Realist later. This stereotype is immensely old. Or we may reverse it, acting in youth as realistic rebels who have seen through the fuddy-duddy moral nonsense offered by their parents – a role which is specially attractive in a rapidly changing age.

Plato displayed this drama shrewdly in the *Gorgias*. Socrates there meets a sharp young politician named Callicles, an immoralist who gives a striking impression of having just read Nietzsche, Machiavelli and the latest postmodern treatments of ethics.... Actually, as it turns out, Callicles hasn't been reading anybody, because (as he explains) he radically despises all theoretical discussion. Thought and argument, he says, are occupations for boys, games to limber up little minds for the real world. Adult life is also a game but it is a serious one, violent and final, a power game to be played as hard as possible for one's own hand. Anyone who gets distracted from it by considerations of truth or consistence, let alone of other people's interests, is obviously a fool.

Callicles, of course, is still with us today. In him, the division between Realist and Idealist, between thought and action, is unusually drastic. He claims to throw ideals overboard entirely (though it is noticeable that he is often gripped by fantasies). More commonly, perhaps, people accept that both aspects of life are necessary but divide the labour, expecting one set of citizens to supply the ideals and another to carry them out. This drama can be played either between the generations or between the sexes. The women can have the ideals while the men take the action. Or, in a democracy, the voters shout their horror at current iniquities and force the administrators – who themselves have no moral views – to make the practical changes. The politicians then form a sort of gear-mechanism connecting the two sides, linking the ideals with reality.

Up to a point these arrangements do work. But they waste a fearful amount of energy in friction and, as we know, there is something really awkward about them. Two parties cannot easily work harmoniously together if they regard each other as (respectively) fools and knaves. That is not a satisfactory principle for any division of labour.

Ideals are not Inert

Should we perhaps suspect, then, that the game was wrongly set up in the first place? Perhaps the two sides of our nature ought not to have got separated? Perhaps, in fact, Realism and Idealism are not alternatives but inseparable aspects of any true practical attitude? But our unlucky tendency to divide them is strong. It is shown, rather comically, in the common saying that some proposal is 'all right in theory but no good in practice'. Such a proposal has surely got something wrong with it in theory too. Theories that do not fit the facts are bad theories and need changing.

This whole question is important to those of us, including students, who spend our time doing intellectual work, some of us actually being paid to do it. Is our occupation with theoretical questions really just a self-contained factory of idle dreams, fantasies and wish-fulfilments? Or are there also dreams which are not idle? Are there *effective* dreams?

Glancing round, it seems plain that there are. The world is changing very fast, and evidently certain dreams – some of them very bad dreams – play a large part in directing that change. An obvious example at present is the monetarist dream that promises us universal prosperity through 'trickle-down' from the uncontrolled working of the markets. This dream has not grown up on its own, like a weed. Its seed was deliberately sown by theorists, by Social Darwinist dreamers in the last century. Their theories were, of course, in part a response to temporary conditions in the real

world – to the early successes of capitalism. But they also flowed from an unbalanced, idealistic excitement about the idea of freedom itself. This excitement did not just distort economies but also made people feel justified in exalting economics into a general guide to life, a guide divorced from social responsibility. And these theories clearly went on to have a profound influence on further changes. In fact, even the most cynical and disastrous doctrines usually do owe some of their strength to one-sided idealism of this kind.

Anyone who has the habit of dismissing ideals, and thoughts about them, as idle – 'all right in theory but ineffective in practice' – is not living in today's world. Only in very stagnant times can current practice be treated as something eternal, a rock upon which the waves of theory will never make any impression. Today, practices as well as theories are in constant transition.

Things *do* change, and among the factors which change them, the accepted ideals of the day always play a central part. The imaginative visions that figure in books, films and TV programmes are not just froth on the surface of the waves or pieces in a game. They have their effect; they can mean life or death, salvation or destruction. Yet the kind of reality that they portray is singularly hard to grasp. We usually oscillate between taking these visions seriously and treating them as a dream. It is when we see them as a dream that we drift into a kind of fatalism, into believing that the practical world is indeed immutable, armoured against all thought.

This fatalism is itself surely just one more rather ineffective emotional defence, a way of avoiding the idea that there is still something we might do. That defence separates the practical from the reflective side of our nature, keeping them apart as chemists separate substances that may explode if they come together. We leave these two aspects chronically at odds and let them take turns at influencing action. Thus, most of us respond sometimes to other people's cynical fatalism with idealistic protests and sometimes to other people's ideals with fatalistic ones.

Is Dialectic Useful?

Might all this opposition be a useful dialectic, producing a synthesis in the end? Some philosophers have said so. But then philosophers do tend to be argumentative people and they sometimes exaggerate the usefulness of conflict. Often, debating only makes the gap between the disputants wider. Each opponent then becomes more divided internally, practising the two roles separately without bringing them together. And when the debate is internalised and thus unacknowledged, there can be no useful dialectic at all.

It is this division, not the outside difficulties, which can finally paralyse us, making us give up thought altogether. And even if the paralysis is not complete, it can still poison our responses. When the side of ourselves that we officially disown has not been properly dealt with, it still causes trouble within us. There is still cognitive dissonance – unresolved confusion in our thought and ambivalence in our feeling. This distorts the way in which we carry on controversies. It can make us violently unfair to our opponents, who stand for the rejected element. And it fixes the idea of a deep warfare between thought and feeling at the heart of our thinking.

The Unseen Campaigners

What can we do about all this? I have been suggesting that the idea of the impotence of thought is just one more myth among others, an image that we devise chiefly as our defence against the exhausting business of confronting reality. This myth is remarkably selective. Its contrast between thought and action lines up, in the oddest manner, with the division between virtue and vice. This myth belongs to Callicles, who lurks inside most of us. It says that iniquity is effective in

the world, while virtue is not, even though iniquity works through our consciousness just as much as virtue does.

Here again, of course, there is a painful half-truth; one so painful and so much neglected that it can easily be mistaken for realism. There is indeed plenty of iniquity about. A great deal of human behaviour is so appalling that we try hard to forget about it. But when we have said this, realism calls on our bewildered imaginations to look further. The other half of this truth is the huge effort that people make to fight against these iniquities. As the Book of Ecclesiasticus puts it:

> *Let us now praise famous men, and our fathers that begat us...*
> *All these were honoured in their generations, and were the glory of their times.*
> *But some there be which have no memorial, which are perished as though they had never been, and their children after them,*
> *And these were merciful men, whose righteousness hath not been forgotten.*
> *There bodies are buried in peace, but their name liveth for evermore.*
>
> *Chapter 44, verses 1-14*

We take all this effort for granted. But when those struggling people happen to relax their energies, we quickly see how much worse things could easily be.

This well-known fact that 'things could be a lot worse' is not just an idle cliché. It is a vital piece of truth. Human history, bad though it is, is still the product of continuous conflict, a constant struggle between worse and better. If you look at it from the devil's point of view (as C S Lewis does in the *Screwtape Letters*) you see that vice does not actually have things all its own way. We overlook this modest fact because of our bitter disappointment that virtue has not achieved more than it has. That recognition realism does demand of us. We are right to be disappointed – right, in a way, to be horrified, by the state of the world. But our disappointment and horror don't licence fatalism.

The balance is really difficult here. There is a fierce tension between ideals and reality, especially, of course, for people who are trying to do something to bridge the gap. Again, this is nothing new. Two thousand years ago Cicero, who was desperately attempting reform but depended on very corrupt allies, cried out that 'the trouble is that we have to work, not in Plato's *Republic* but in Romulus's pigsty'.

In this mood, it is natural to write off all expressions of ideals, including books like the *Republic*, as simply irrelevant to reality. But this very natural response misses the point. We have to have this longer perspective – the perspective that includes ideals – if we are to make sense of what is immediately before us. These distant visions are an essential part of the scene. They form its necessary background. If we try to work with a world-view which shows us nothing but the present horror and complexity, we lose our bearings altogether and forget where we are going. By their very nature, ideals have to be remote from practice. A society ruled by ideals which were no better than its current practice would be in an absurd condition. This remoteness does not mean at all that the ideals have no influence.

And of course, deliberately limited views that are supposed to be realistic are not actually realistic either. They are as selective as any other view of the facts. Every account enshrines some particular emphases and expresses some dream. All are shaped by our value-judgements, our particular fears and ideals. That is why human imagination needs to be stimulated, not from one point on this spectrum, but from many. If we are to keep our power of responding to what goes on, we need to be struck constantly from different angles by different aspects of the truth. We need to consult many conceptual maps – many attitudes, many ideologies – and be ready to use one to correct and supplement another.

Pluralism is not Nihilism

Recently some 'postmodern' theorists have travestied this need for plurality of angles by recommending a mere lack of conviction, a kind of all-purpose sceptical 'irony' which is too sophisticated ever to commit itself to treating anything as true. This gets the point upside-down. The reason why we must be open to many kinds of message is not that none of them are true, but that they are all partially true.

'The whole truth' is indeed a distant ideal for us, like a signpost saying 'To the North' rather than one saying 'To Edinburgh'. But eliminating wrong answers to questions does really move us truthwards. The concept of truth has indeed got its difficulties, but they arise mainly over attempts to fit it into over-ambitious philosophical theories about knowledge. In its ordinary uses, truth is not an obscure idea because its meaning, like that of some other large words, is made clear by its opposites. Falsehood, error and deception are central factors in our lives. If we fix our eyes on them, we can see well enough what we can reasonably mean by truth.

Any serious attempt to dispense with the idea of truth would land us, not just in mild irony, but in a detachment from life which is literally inconceivable. We ourselves are still part of this complex world. We cannot withdraw from it into a safe, elegant, all-round scepticism. We are not detached spectators on another planet writing doctoral theses about terrestrial affairs. Inadequate though our information is, we have to come off fences and form opinions that we can act on. We must make choices.

Many of these choices are not obscure at all. It is not (for instance) obscure whether we ought to allow the torturing of prisoners or the destruction of irreplaceable natural resources. But many big questions arising today really are obscure, partly because they are questions about choices of evils – for instance, about weighing local needs against wider ones, present needs against the future, current human prosperity against the survival of the habitat – and partly because the world has changed so fast that many of them are new. Long-term prediction, indeed, often seems impossible.

In this painful situation, people find simple formulas hugely comforting, which is why governments throughout the world tend at present to clasp the tenets of economics to their bosoms like a charm. Although it is clear, if you think about it, that economics can provide neither a general way of comparing values nor a formula for predicting facts – although you cannot eat money – although 'economic man' is well known to be an unreal abstraction and nobody even tries to believe in 'economic woman' – although, in fact, economics deals only with a limited set of exchanges and has never claimed to be a general guide to life, yet economics is quantitative, it looks like an all-purpose measure. It therefore seems capable of saving officials from the responsibility of seriously weighing one evil against another so as to judge reasonably what actually needs to be done next.

Formula-bound thinking of this sort imprisons the imagination. It stops us using what we know to be the great asset of our species – human versatility. If we are to free ourselves from such formulas our imagination needs many sorts of nourishment and stimuli. Among them it certainly needs art. Most of art does not, of course, deal explicitly and directly with our practical dilemmas. But all art embodies visions, and our visions express the ideals that move us. If we are to avoid dropping into fatalistic resignation that glues us to our existing grooves, we need constantly to drink at this spring, to renew our contact with these visions. Though art can be used for escape from reality, it is not in its essence an escape. It is the necessary nourishment of effective idealism.

8

BRIDGING CIVILISATIONS

Saad Eddin Ibrahim

Until the summer of 1993, we as Arab Muslim Third Worlders used to lament the sensational Western media for its gross oversimplification and distortions of our complex realities at home. However, those of us who lived or were educated in the West, could excuse such oversimplification because the inner dynamics and time imperatives of the Western electronic media industry.

But when a renowned American political scientist, Samuel Huntington, writes in the prestigious *Foreign Affairs* about 'The Clash of Civilisations'(Summer 1993), in a manner not so different from that of the mass media, the matter becomes a cause for serious alarm. Huntington's article borders on the quest for a search for a 'New Enemy' of the West in the post-Cold War era. In the words of a critic in the same journal:

> *Huntington has found his civilisations whole and intact, watertight under an eternal sky. Buried alive, as it were, during the years of the Cold War, these civilisations (Islamic, Confucian, Japanese, Hindu, etc...) rose as soon as the stone was rolled off, dusted themselves off, and proceeded to claim the loyalty of their adherents.*

(Ajami, F 'The Summoning')

The most damning of Huntington's points is the 'Battle Cry' conclusion, 'the paramount axis of world politics will be "the West and the Rest…." The central focus of conflict for the immediate future will be between the West and several Islamic-Confucian states.' He goes on to delineate the ways and means of managing this conflict by subduing Muslims and Confucian states.

I have no intention of taking issue with Huntington's propositions. Suffice it to say that what he has done in 'The Clash of Civilisations' is to engage in *cultural stereotyping* and/or *ethnocentrism*, from which we as sociologists have been trained to refrain.

What I will do, instead, is to say something briefly about stereotyping as a concept long studied by sociologists and social psychologists. Then, I will take a look with you at a fragment of Western history which bears a stunning resemblance to some of what the Arab-Muslim world is going through today. This will entail an account of what seems to have frightened Huntington and many of his contemporaries in the West at present – Islamic activism.

I will conclude with a plea for a serious disaggregation of the complex and simultaneous socio-political processes now unfolding in the Arab-Muslim world. It is a renowned plea for *cultural relativism*, a requisite for the bridging, not the clashing, of civilisations. After all, cultural relativism is the diametrical opposite of cultural stereotypes. Both are collective mental constructs – ie they germinate in the minds of humans. But while one leads to understanding, compassion, and cooperation, the other leads to misunderstanding, hate, and conflict.

As we all know, stereotypes are categorical beliefs about groups, peoples, nations, even whole civilisations. Stereotypes are invariably generalised, inaccurate and resistant to new information or empirical testing. Stereotypes are *ahistorical*, *absolutist* cultural constructs. In this sense, stereotypes are the causal ingredients and effects of prejudices, racism and discrimination. The worst aspect of all this is the possibility of *self-fulfilling prophecies* – ie a group perceived to act in a stereotypical manner by another is subjected to treatment which makes it respond in ways concordant with the stereotype!

The Western stereotypes of the Arab-Muslim world are a case in point. To start with, not all Arabs are Muslims and not all Muslims are Arabs. Yet the two are often lumped together and judged as irrational, violent, rigid, fanatical, and anti-Western. Second, not all Arabs are the same – except in so much as all Europeans (Russians, French and Danes) are the same. Nor are all Muslims (eg Indonesians, Moroccans and Bosnians) are the same – except in so much as all Christians are the same (eg Filipinos, Italians, Swedes and Irish). In other words, stereotyping peoples and countries of the Arab-Muslim world not only ignores the nuances of variation but also the major differences.

I will attempt to demystify contemporary Islamic activism in as many of its facets as possible. My message here is simple. Political Islam has always been an idiom for expressing profound worldly grievances and the quest for the good life here on earth. Like radicals everywhere throughout history, Islamic radicals moderate once accommodated and incorporated into the socio-political mainstream. If radicals do not moderate in time, they perish or become sociologically irrelevant cults.

Let me demonstrate my argument by examining a chapter from Western history. On 25 February 1534, in the German town of Munster, Anabaptist zealots staged an armed uprising and installed a radical dictatorship. All who refused to undergo rebaptism into the new faith were driven from the city without food or belongings during a snowstorm. The regime impounded all food, money and valuables and cancelled all debt. Mobs burned the financial records of all local merchants. The housing of the fleeing well-to-do was reassigned to the poor. Former beggars capered in the streets, decked in plundered finery. The religious positions of the new regime were equally radical. Under the new moral order it imposed, all books other than the Bible were burned. All 'sins', including swearing, backbiting, complaining and disobedience, were to be punished by instant execution. Soon the regime instituted polygamy. Unmarried women were ordered to marry the first man who asked them – and 49 women were executed and their bodies hacked into quarters for failing to comply. Before long, however, the outside world reacted. Munster was soon besieged by its Bishop who had escaped and recruited an army of mercenaries. Surrounded and cut off, the city was beset by growing confusion. Then, out of the rebel ranks there arose a new and absolute leader – John Bockelson, who assumed the name of John of Leyden and claimed to have been appointed by God to be king of the last days. A 'this-worldly' rebellion now became firmly 'other-worldly'. The rebels did not need to win victory over their temporal rulers, for all was now in the hands of God in these last days before the Last Judgement, announced by John of Leyden to be coming before Easter 1535. Anyone in Munster who opposed or expressed doubts about this prophecy was executed. On 24 June 1535, the Bishop's troops made a surprise assault in the night and took the city. John of Leyden was arrested. Over the next few months, he was led by a chain from town to town, and in January 1536 led back to Munster, where he was tortured to death with hot red irons in front of a large crowd. His body was put in an iron cage and suspended from the church tower. The cage still hangs there today. (For a full account, see Stark, R and Williams Bainbridge (1985) *The Future of Religion: Secularization, Revival and Cult Formation,* University of California Press.)

There was nothing very unusual about the rebellion in Munster, or that it took the form of a religious movement.

Similar events were commonplace in Europe at the time, especially in the growing commercial towns. The few decades preceding and following the Munster episode were replete with intense 'worldly' discontent, shrouded in religious discourse and conflict, as a quick glance at the annals of the first half of the 16th century would substantiate. Eighteen years before the Munster uprising, Sir Thomas More wrote his *Utopia* (1516). A year later (1517), in protest against the sale of 'indulgences', Martin Luther posted his 95 theses on the door of Palast Church in Wittenberg, marking the beginning the Reformation. Actually by the time of the Munster rebellion, Martin Luther had completed the first translation of the Bible into German, and two years later he had his 'Table Talks'. Two years after the execution of John of Leyden, Calvin was expelled from Geneva to settle in Strasbourg. In 1542, Pope Paul II established the Inquisition in Rome, and a year later, the first Protestants were burned at the stake in Spain. In 1544, Pope Paul II called a general council at Trent. The Council met a year later to discuss Reformation and Counter-Reformation.

This was a period of great transformations ushered in by the dramatic geographic explorations, scientific discoveries and sprouting capitalism of those times. By the time of the Munster uprising the Americas had been discovered. Some 25 universities had been founded all over Europe. The printing press had already turned out some 10 million copies of published books in various European languages. Before the mid-16th century, religious reformation and counter-reformation would sweep Germany, France, Switzerland, England, Scotland, Poland, Spain and Sweden.

Viewing 16th century Europe in retrospect is very instructive to understanding what is happening in the Arab Muslim world in the late 20th century. The so-called Islamic revival is as much an expression of 'worldly' concern as it is a religious quest for 'other-worldly' salvation.

The seizure of the Grand Mosque of Mecca at the end of 1979 by a group of Muslim zealots led by a young man, Juhiman al-Qutiabi, resembles in many ways the Munster rebellion. The leader and his followers were all in their twenties and early thirties. They were of Bedouin tribal origin, newcomers to the rapid urbanising centres of Saudi Arabia. In their youthful lifetime they had already witnessed the profound, but confusing, socio-economic transformation of their country resulting from the oil boom. In the ten years preceding their rebellion, Saudi Arabia had doubled its total population, tripled its urban population, and increased its money wealth ten-fold. There were as many expatriates as native Saudis. The expatriates poured into the country in unprecedented numbers, especially after 1973; they came from as many and as far lands as Korea, Australia, Scandinavia and America. While Saudis may have been used to Arabs and Muslims coming in for the pilgrimage, the oil boom waves of expatriates had nothing or very little in common with the Saudi natives. Different in languages, religions and lifestyles, the expatriates were running much of the economic life of Saudi Arabia. Meanwhile, the sudden wealth from skyrocketing oil prices was hardly equitably distributed. Nor was political power equitably shared. Estrangement or alienation of Saudis in their own country was growing as rapidly as the oil wealth in those years. Like youth elsewhere, young Saudis, especially those with some education, felt the brunt of such estrangement more than others. With restricted participation in socio-economic life because of limited skills and training for modern institutions to be built, and with no political participation under the autocratic repressive Saudi regime, long allied with the religious monopoly of the *Wahaabi* establishment, young Juhiman al-Qutiabi and his fellow zealots must have felt the same way as John of Leyden four and a half centuries earlier. The end result was nearly the same. The Grand Mosque of Mecca was soon besieged by Saudi government troops. The needed pronouncements of condemnation were quickly issued by Sheikh Ben-Baz, the head of the *Wahaabi* establishment. However, unable to persuade the rebels to surrender and with the Saudi troops unable to storm the Grand Mosque, the Saudi regime called on French mercenaries to do the job. Several of the zealot Brothers were killed in the process; others arrested, quickly tried and beheaded. The uprising was crushed. The whole episode ended in three weeks.

Two similar episodes, though different in detail, had taken place in Egypt in 1974 and 1977, and one in Tunisia just a few months before the Grand Mosque seizure (in 1979). The zealots were not the poorest of the poor, nor were they the 'scum' misfits of the earth. They were all young and among the relatively better educated in their societies. They were all newcomers to the big city from tribal and rural origins. Like their counterparts in Munster, their *tocsin* was against King and Pope. In the Arab-Muslim world, that reads as repressive political regimes and allied religious establishment. The counter weapon of Islamic zealots is equally a combination of the political and the religious.

More than Christianity, and other religions, Islam lends itself as a mobilising political weapon. In its precepts and dicta, Islam is as much 'worldly' as 'other-worldly'. In the latter it promises a glorious life on earth to the believers who adhere to its teachings in letter and spirit. Hence the battle cry of today's activists: 'Islam is the Solution'. The idealised history which Muslims learn in school and hear about in Mosques has a simple uni-dimensional message: Islam in the days of the Prophet Mohammed and the Guided Caliphs enabled Muslims to be virtuous, just, prosperous and strong. The true believers conquered the world and built the greatest civilisation humanity had ever known. When Muslims strayed away from the straight path of Islam, they became decadent, poor and weak. The culprits are sinful rulers at home and enemies of Islam abroad. To restore on earth the 'paradise lost', it is the duty of every good Muslim to strive by deeds and words to restore the true Islamic societal-moral order. Striving mainly by 'deeds' is what sets Islamic activists apart from other Muslims. Acting on such beliefs is what puts some of them in lethal confrontations, not only with their respective states and regimes, but also often against the rest of their societies.

The first Muslim state of Medina, set up by the Prophet Mohammed and his four Guided Caliphs (successors), lasted for only forty years (AD 622–661). For the following fourteen centuries, the imagination of successive generations of Muslims has been galvanised by the purified glorious tales of those four decades. The history of Muslims since AD 661 is replete with socio-religious movements in quest for the 'paradise lost'. Not all such movements succeeded in seizing power; and none managed to restore the 'paradise lost'. The political success and religious failure had always sown the seeds of new socio-religious movements.

Ibn Khaldoun, the great Arab thinker, noted the cyclicity and the success prerequisites of such movements which enabled them to seize political power and establish dynasties of their own. According to him, it is always an *asabiya* (esprit de corps) and a 'religious mission'. The *asabiya*, often embodied in a strong tribe or a tribal coalition, provides the muscles of political-military success. The religious mission provides the spiritual raison d'être and legitimacy for success. To put it another way, the movement had to provide an alternative 'King and Pope', to a decaying King and Pope. The last literal manifestations of the Khaldounian paradigm were in the nineteenth century; the *Saudi-Wahaabi* movement in the Arabian Peninsula; the Sanusi movement in North Africa, and the *Mahadist* movement in the Sudan.

In Khaldounian times, the would-be movement-tribe was often in the hinterland, at an unreachable distance from the seat of political power. That hinterland was dubbed *bilad al-Siba* or the unruly country – in contrast to *bilad al Maghzin*, or the ruly and tax-paying country. As the central power weakened, the *siba* country expanded and inched closer to the capital until the right moment for the coup de grace against a decaying ruling elite. A new 'tribe-dynasty', legitimised and empowered by a religious vision, takes over to restore the Islamic lost paradise. The rest of the cycle unfolds over three to four generations, until another *siba* hinterland tribe and another religious vision coalesce into a new movement.

This elegant *Khaldounian* paradigm accounted for much, if not all, of medieval Arab-Muslim history. With socio-cultural changes and growing integration into a world system, the paradigm no longer accounts for the march of Arab-Muslim history. But some of its internal logic may still be operative. The mobilising power of an Islamic vision in quest

of the 'paradise lost' still appeals to the marginals, the relatively deprived, and the powerless.

In this century, the 'tribe' alone may no longer be a viable organisational base for a socio-religious movement, although in recent Yemeni elections (1993), we note an alliance between the *Hashid* tribe and the Islamic *Islah* (Reform) Party. More often, however, it is now an 'underclass' which substitutes for tribe in fuelling socio-religious movements in the Arab-Muslim world. Algeria and Egypt are striking cases in point. In both, one-party populist regimes ruled for 30–40 years before they were forcefully challenged by sprouting Islamic movements.

Initially, the single-party populist regimes had an attractive vision of their own. The vision promised tremendous worldly rewards: consolidation of newly gained independence, rapid development, economic prosperity, social justice and cultural authenticity. Though not quite paradise on earth, the populist vision promised something very close to it. There were implicit conditions, however, for delivering on the populist promises: the 'masses' were to work hard without demanding liberal political participation. With no previous firm traditions of participatory governance anyhow, this populist trade-off formula seemed acceptable to the vast majority. For the first decade or two, the populist social contract seemed to be working. Remarkable expansion in education, industrialisation, health and provision of other services were effected. With these real gains, a new middle class and a modern working class grew steadily under state tutelage.

However, there were unintended adverse consequences of populist policies: rapid growth of population, urbanisation and bureaucratisation. In the first twenty years of Algeria's populist regime (1962–1982), its population had doubled, its urbanisation tripled, and its bureaucracy quadrupled. In Egypt it took slightly longer – about 27 to 30 years. By the third decade of populist rule, the regimes in both countries were no longer able to effectively manage their society and state. A new socio-economic formation grew rapidly. For the lack of better than a Marxist term, this was the *urban proletariat* (UP). With high expectations, but little or no employable skills, capital, or civic norms, the swarming millions of rural newcomers to the cities made up the UP. They crowded the older city quarters or – more often – created their own slum areas. Called *bidonvilles* in Algeria and *ashwaiyat* in Egypt, these densely overpopulated slum areas would become the late 20th century equivalent of the Khaldounian *siba*. Their human stuff is proving to be the most flammable material in Arab-Muslim society today. Its youth is an easy prey for manipulation by demagogues, organised criminals, agents provocateurs and Islamic activists.

To make things worse for populist regimes, the lower rungs of the new middle class were steadily alienated by dwindling opportunities for employment or upward social-mobility, began a mass desertion. From their ranks Islamic activists would sprout and manipulate the UP of the new *siba* in staging their challenge vis-à-vis the now ageing and decaying populist ruling elite.

To use the Khaldounian analogy, a typical armed confrontation between an activist Islamic-led new Siba and the Egyptian state (new *maghazin*) took place in December 1992. By official figures, some 700 shanty areas (*ashwaiyat*) have sprung up in or around Egypt's major urban centres over the last two decades. Their total population is estimated between 8 and 10 million. Western Munira is one such area. Located on the north-western edge of Imbaba in Greater Cairo, it is less than three kilometres across the Nile from the aristocratic upper class district of Zamalek (residential area of most of the *maghazin* elite). One-tenth the territorial size of Zamalek, Western Munira has ten times its population. With nearly 100 times the population density of Zamalek, dwellers had no schools, hospitals, sewage system, public transportation, or police stations within walking distance. For many years, Western Munira represented a 'Hobbesian world', run by thugs, criminals, drug dealers and infested with every known vice. With no state presence, it was also used as a hide-out for many Islamic militants on the run. In the late 1980s, one of them, Sheikh Gaber, felt safe enough to operate in the open. He preached and recruited several followers, and in no time he emerged as a community leader. He began to weed out the vice lords, impose order, the veil, arrange marriages, and collect 'taxes'. The

Egyptian state did not take any notice of him, until a Reuters reporter filed a story about 'Sheikh Gaber, the President of the Republic of Imbaba'. Angered and embarrassed, the Egyptian authorities ordered the reporter out of the country, and staged an armed expedition to arrest Sheikh Gaber. By the official count, some 12,000 armed security forces laid siege to Western Munira, then stormed the place. The operation took three weeks before Sheikh Gaber and 600 of his followers were killed, wounded, or arrested.

Similar confrontations have been frequent in both Egypt and Algeria since 1991. The casualties toll has escalated in Egypt from 96 in 1991 to 322 in 1992, to 1106 in 1993, ie more than a tenfold increase in three years. In Algeria, the toll more than doubled in one year (from 450 in 1992 to 1055 in 1993). A war of attrition is the order of the day in both countries. It is a war between an Islamic-led new *siba* and the state.

The profile comparisons between typical challenger militants and the challenged populist rulers are stark. Of equal or superior formal education, the Islamic militant is at least thirty years younger. Nearly 90 per cent of those militants arrested or killed in armed confrontations with the Algerian state in the last two years were born after independence (1962), ie after the present populist regime came to power. Some of Egypt's militants who were recently arrested, tried and sentenced to death were under 18 years old, ie born after Mubarak came to power (as Vice President in 1975), and after the beginning of the uninterrupted tenure of at least four of his present cabinet members.

Not only did the populist regimes fail to renew their ranks by infusing new blood and new ideas, but worse, for a long time they repressed or circumvented other orderly social forces from sharing the public space. The middle and upper rungs of the middle class, men and women, were not allowed enough margin of freedom to evolve autonomous civil society organisations. Had such a civil society been in place during the period of populist state retreat (the 1970s and 1980s), both Egypt and Algeria could have weathered the Islamic-led new *siba* storm. Egypt nearly stood still with its timid democratisation since the early 1980s. Algeria rushed clumsily into it in the early 1990s.

Surprisingly, what Michael Hudson calls the 'modernising monarchies' of the Arab-Muslim would have been more able to weather the Islamic-led *siba* storms. Different in many ways from their populist neighbours, Arab modernising monarchies in Morocco and Jordan faced similar socio-economic structural problems during the 1980s, eg a growing population, urbanisation, bureaucratisation, huge external debt, and shrinking state resource base. They had their share of new *siba* food rioting in the 1980s. But instead of repression, dragging or rushing, the two monarchies engineered an orderly gradual democratisation. They initiated public debates on governance and constitutional issues in which all political forces participated. A 'national pact' or a 'new social contract' was implicitly or explicitly formulated. Municipal and parliamentary elections were held, with a marked degree of fairness. The secular opposition in Morocco and the Islamic forces in Jordan won an impressive number of seats. Women were elected to national parliaments for the first time in both countries.

Morocco and Jordan are not, and may not for a long time, be constitutional monarchies. Nor are there any illusions about their parliamentary experiments of governance becoming a Westminster-style democracy in the near future. But their socio-political march in the last five years has been far more orderly than that of Algeria and Egypt. There has been no politically motivated violence, killing or rioting in either country. Islamic militancy hardly exists in Morocco, and is fairly tamed or under control in Jordan.

In Kuwait (1992), Lebanon (1992), and Yemen (1993), Islamists participated in parliamentary elections. They came second in Kuwait and Yemen, and had an impressive showing in winning several of the seats assigned to both Shiite and Sunni Muslims in Lebanon. Even in Egypt, though not officially recognised as a legal party, the Muslim Brothers ran for parliamentary elections under the banner of other parties in 1984 (with the Wafd) and in 1987 (with the Labour Socialist Party). In both elections, the Muslim Brothers won several seats and came out in third place among nine

contending parties.

Beyond the Arab world, Islamists have regularly run for elections in Pakistan, and since the mid-1980s in Indonesia and the Islamic republics of the former Soviet Union. Islamists have been peacefully engaged in local and municipal politics and petitioning for recognition and expansion of pluralistic politics on the national level.

There are a number of lessons to be drawn from the contrasting cases of Algeria and Egypt on the one hand and the rest of the Arab-Muslim world on the other.

First, political Islam has grown and spread in the last two decades as an idiom of protest against repression, social injustice and the threat to collective identity. Its radicalism is commensurate with the degree to which these ills are felt or perceived by the young educated Muslims. Political Islam has not been the only vision appealing to Muslims. The Arab-Muslims had responded strongly to other secular visions in this century, eg Arab nationalism, and inter-war liberalism.

Second, despite their initial radical messages and/or actions, Islamic militants are tameable through accommodative politics of inclusion. Runing for office, or once in it, they recognise the complexities of the real world and the need for gradualism and toleration. The 'worldly' increasingly inches on the 'other worldly' in their consciousness, language and actions. Starting as a 'pro-natalist', Iran's Islamic Revolution is now feverishly pursuing an 'anti-natalist' population policy. In this respect, Islamic activists are no different from their Chinese communist counterparts.

Third, people in Muslim societies, like people everywhere, may give new visions and promised solutions a chance when the old ones fail. But at the end of the day, they judge the new ones by their concrete results. The Islamists in Jordan lost one-third of the number of seats between the 1989 and 1993 elections. Despite the majority of seats won in the last aborted parliamentary elections, Algeria's Islamic Salvation Front (FIS) lost one million net votes between 1990 and 1991. In both Jordan and Algeria, the initial flare of the 'Islamic Alternative' lost some of its glare once Islamists were tried in office.

Fourth, peoples of the Muslim world have increasingly been integrated into the international system. The radical Islamists among them can not ignore this fact. Even their anti-Western rhetoric is an idiom of protest against worldly grievances. Once fairly or equitably addressed, cooperation becomes not only possible, but also desirable. In this respect, Islamic radicals are no different from their nationalist counterparts of an earlier generation. The problem of Muslim peoples with the West is like their problems with their own repressive corrupt regimes. Not only does the legacy of Western colonialism lurk in Muslems' collective memory, but it is easily invoked with every contemporary Western act or policy which smacks of double standards. Recently, the reaction of the West to the massacres of Muslims by non-Muslims in marketplaces in Bosnia or mosques in Palestine seemed muted at best. Equally, Algeria's short-lived experiment with pluralistic politics was a test of whether Islamists could reconcile with democracy. But it was as much a test of whether the West could reconcile with Muslim democracy. The West has long been on the best of terms with Muslim despots, eg Saudi Arabia, the Gulf, Iran's Shah, and Pakistan's Zia'ul-Haq.

Fifth, as a thoughtful Western observer recently noted, Islamic societies now find themselves in the opening rounds of what the West went through in the 16th and 17th centuries in redefining both the relationship between God and Man, among human beings, and between them and the state (Wright, Robin 'Islam, Democracy, and the West' *Foreign Affairs*, Summer 1992). We believe that Muslim society will emerge from this process more rational and more democratic. The process, however, could be much shorter and less costly if the West lends an honest hand on the side of democratic forces. The West has recently been interfering militarily in the affairs of Muslim societies – from Libya to Somalia, and from the Gulf to Kurdistan. It has also been doing so as much economically, directly or through the IMF/World Bank prescribed structural adjustment policies. The West is yet to do the same politically for democracy. Even if

it brings into office some radical Islamists, they would soon lose either their 'radicalism' or 'Islamism'. Muslims everywhere have taken note that the Islamic Afghani *Mujahidin* are fighting each other for worldly gains (power), as their counterparts had previously done in post-Shah's Iran. Muslims recognise that the Islamists are not saints. But they may be less devilish than their present old repressive rulers.

I conclude with a plea to all social scientists and humanists alike to continue to engage in a serious disaggregation of the complex processes now unfolding in various regions of the world.

It is a renewed plea for the rehabilitation of the concepts of cultural diversity and the practice of 'cultural relativism' as a requisite for the 'bridging' not the 'clashing' of civilisations. Boundaries will always exist so long as human groups continue to exist. But they need not be hostile boundaries. We need neither another Great Wall of China nor another Berlin Wall. Neither wall stood the test of time. Their remnants in China and Germany are now sheer tourist attractions. Let us hope that Samuel Huntington's Clash of Civilisations will not turn out to be a self-fulfilling prophecy, but simply an intellectual tourist attraction.

The Right to Hope project has the same message. It takes human beings to be the heart of the universe. It recognises both their 'needs' and their 'greed'. It takes from the Ghandian principle that our universe has enough for all mankind's needs, but not for their greed. It is the latter which has plunged humanity into war, racism, exploitation, and is threatening the environment.

The Right to Hope project recognises that hope is the engine of change. But for that change to be guided by wisdom and compassion, a relentless striving to inform and enlighten public opinion must be maintained. This paper has tried to do just that, ie to show that the young people of the Arab-Muslim world are not different from others in their legitimate aspirations for a dignified life. To the extent that they are treated with compassion and understanding, they will ultimately reciprocate in kind. To the extent that they find legitimate channels which equitably reward their hard work, they will exert themselves to the maximum. To the extent that the propositions of freedom, justice and security are universalised for all, the people of the Arab-Muslim world will join enthusiastically, as they have often done in the past, in building a better global order.

9

MONOCULTURES, MONOPOLIES AND THE MASCULINISATION OF KNOWLEDGE

Vandana Shiva

In the words of Francis Bacon, the birth of modern science was also 'The Masculine Birth of Time'. Thus the fathers of modern science viewed their particular approaches to knowledge as essentially gendered and masculine.

As Brian Easlea has recalled in *Science and Sexual Oppression*, (Wildenfeld and Nicholson, 1981) Francis Bacon appealed to the 'true sons of knowledge' to find a way into nature's 'inner chambers' by turning their 'united forces against the nature of things, to storm and occupy her castles and strongholds'

Susan Bordo in 'The Cartesian Masculinisation of Thought' (*Sex and Scientific Inquiry*, University of Chicago Press, 1987) has proposed that the project of modern science crystallises 'masculinist' modes of thinking. The scientific model of knowledge, says Sandra Harding in the same book, represents a 'super-masculinisation' of rational knowledge.

This does not imply that men essentially think in this way, but that the masculine mind that discards part of its own faculties as 'feminine' and 'inferior' creates a particular consciousness that is gendered as masculine. Ways of thinking are not biologically determined but culturally shaped. The masculinisation of knowledge is a cultural project initiated by European men who are called the fathers of modern science. I will not dwell on how early modern science was seen as gendered by its fathers, but how it is being freshly gendered in our times.

The three aspects unique to modern science are:

1. *its intrinsic reductionism and fragmentation;*
2. *its separation of the knower and the knowledge; and*
3. *its union with economic power.*

The first aspect of reductionism has led to the destruction of diversity and the emergence of what I have called 'monocultures of the mind'. The second and third aspects have led to the creation of a monopoly in knowledge, the latest manifestation of which are 'intellectual property rights'. Monocultures and monopolies in the field of agriculture are vivid examples of the masculinisation of knowledge.

MONOCULTURES AS AN EXPRESSION OF RACE, CLASS AND GENDER

In the fields of Third World women farmers, the most conspicuous characteristic is the diversity of crops. We have named our agricultural biodiversity conservation programme Navdanya, which means nine seeds. Navdanya is a system of polyculture as well as a microcosm representing the complexity of the cosmos.

In the rainfed areas, a particular cropping pattern takes place called baranaja – which means, literally, twelve seeds. The seeds of twelve different crops (often more than twelve, never less than twelve) are mixed and then sown randomly in a field which is fertilised with cow dung and farmyard manure.

Care is taken to balance the distribution of the twelve crops in each area of the field. Thus, after sowing, the farmer is required to transplant crops from one area of the field to another in order to maintain an even distribution. As in other cultivation practices, constant weeding is necessary. All the crops are sown in May, but are harvested at different times, from late August to early November, thus ensuring a continuous food supply for the farmer during this period and beyond. The twelve different crops have been selected by the farmers over the ages by observing certain relationships between plant and plant, and between plant and soil. For example, the rajma creeper will climb only on the marsha plant and on no other plant in the field. This cultivation practice was almost irreversibly lost but has been reintroduced at Navdanya's demonstration and propagation centre. Farmers from neighbouring villages have since reintroduced this cultivation practice in their own villages. What the baranaja field displays is biodiversity as relational, rather than arithmetic or numeric.

The relationship between different plants leads to symbiosis, which contributes towards increased crop productivity. Assessments made at the conservation centre show that if farmers cultivate baranaja, they get higher yields and diverse outputs. Cultivating diversity can therefore be part of a farming strategy for high yields and high incomes. Since these yields are of diverse crops, centralised commercial interests are not interested in them. For them, uniformity and monocultures are an imperative. However, from the point of view of small farmers, diversity is both highly productive and sustainable.

The freedom for diverse species and ecosystems to organise themselves is the basis of ecology. Ecological stability derives from the ability of species and ecosystems to adapt, evolve and respond. In fact, the higher the degree of freedom available to a system, the more scope for self-organisation that system will have. External control reduces the degrees of freedom a system has and reduces its capacity to organise and renew itself.

Ecological vulnerability stems from the fact that species and ecosystems have been engineered and controlled to such an extent that they have lost their capacity to adapt. The Chilean scientists, Maturana and Varela, have distinguished between two kinds of systems – *autopoietic* and *allopoietic*. A system is autopoietic when its function is primarily geared to self renewal. An autopoietic system is self-referential. In contrast, an allopoietic system, such as a machine, refers to a function given from outside, such as the production of a specific output.

- Self-organising systems grow from within. They shape themselves from within outwards. Externally organised mechanical systems do not grow, they are made.

- Self-organising systems are distinct and multi-dimensional. They therefore display structural and functional diversity. Mechanical systems are uniform and one-dimensional.

- Self-organising systems can heal themselves and adapt to changing environmental conditions. Mechanically organised systems do not heal or adapt, they break down.

The more complex a dynamic structure is, the more endogenously it is driven. Its changes depend not only on its external compulsions, but also on its internal conditions. Self-organisation is the essence of the health and ecological stability of living systems.

When organisms and systems are treated as if they were machines, and are mechanically manipulated to improve a one-dimensional function, including the increase in one-dimensional productivity, either the organisms' immunity can decrease, and it becomes vulnerable to disease and attack by other organisms, or the organism becomes dominant in an ecosystem, and displaces other species, pushing them into extinction. Ecological problems arise from applying the engineering paradigm to life. This paradigm gains yet more impact in the field of genetic engineering, which will have major ecological and ethical implications.

- Diversity is a product of many orders of self-organisation. Varieties of species are distinct because of the self-organisation capacity of living systems.

- Diverse species in partnership and in symbiotic interaction create the self-organisation of polycultures and agricultural ecosystems. Human communities, as part of these agricultural systems, work in partnership with other species to maintain ecological processes and meet human needs.

- Diversity-based agriculture is decentralised, ecologically stable, and economically productive. However, its productivity can only be truly assessed from the perspective of diversity.

The monoculture mind sees polycultures as low yielding and inefficient. Not until diversity is made the logic of production can diversity be conserved. If production continues to be based on the logic of uniformity and homogenisation, uniformity will continue to displace diversity. 'Improvement' from the corporate viewpoint, or from the viewpoint of western agricultural or forestry research, is often a loss for the Third World, especially for the poor in the Third World. There is therefore no inevitability that production should act against diversity. Uniformity as a pattern of production becomes inevitable only in a context of control and profitability.

The spread of monocultures of 'fast-growing species' in forestry and 'high-yielding varieties' in agriculture has been justified on the grounds of increased productivity. All technological transformation of biodiversity is justified in the language of 'improvement' and the increase of 'economic value'. However, 'improvement' and 'value' are not neutral terms. They are contextual and value-laden. Improvement of tree species means one thing for a paper corporation which needs pulping wood, and an entirely different thing for a farmer who needs fodder and green manure. Improvement of crop species means one thing for a processing industry and something totally different for a self-provisioning farmer.

However, categories of 'yield', 'productivity' and 'improvement' which have emerged from the corporate viewpoint have been treated as universal and value-neutral. Thus, all tree-planting programmes financed by international institutions in recent years and encouraged by the Tropical Forestry Action Plan (TFAP) have spread eucalyptus monocultures across Asia, Africa and Latin America. The argument used most frequently in favour of the spread of eucalyptus monocultures is that the tree is fast-growing. However, the only benefit of fast-growth is in terms of wood for other purposes. In terms of yields of non-woody biomass for fodder, eucalyptus has zero yield since its leaves are not eaten by cattle. (Shiva, V and Bandopadhyay, J (1987) *Ecological Audit of Eucalyptus Cultivation*, Research Foundation for Science and Ecology.)

Given that the industrial sector does not benefit from the diversity of species or the diverse uses of trees, forestry programmes deliberately destroy diversity so as to increase yields of industrial raw material. Thus, in spite of high diversity and high productivity of tropical forests which yield up to 300 tons of wood per hectare, as compared to 150 tons per hectare for temperate forests, naturally diverse tropical forests are considered 'unproductive'. Referring to the diversity and large biomass of tropical forests, a forestry expert has stated:

that from a standpoint of industrial material supply, this is relatively unimportant. The important question is how much of this biomass represents trees and parts of trees of preferred species that can be profitably marketed today. By current utilisation standards, most of the trees in these tropical forests are, from an industrial materials standpoint, clearly weeds.
Vandana Shiva (1987) *Forestry Crisis and Forestry Myths* World Rainforest Movement

Viewing diversity as weeds leads to the extinction of that diversity which has high ecological and social values even when it does not profit industry. The pattern of the destruction of diversity has been the same in forestry and agriculture.

Plant improvement in agriculture has been based on the 'enhancement' of the yield of the desired product at the expense of unwanted plant parts. The 'desired' product is however not the same for agribusiness and Third World farmers. Which parts of a farming system will be treated as 'unwanted' depends on one's class and gender. What is unwanted for agribusiness may be wanted by the poor, and by squeezing out those aspects of biodiversity, agriculture 'development' fosters poverty and ecological decline.

In India, the 'high-yielding' strategy of the Green Revolution squeezed out pulses and oilseeds which were essential for nutrition and soil fertility. The monocultures of the dwarf varieties of wheat and rice also squeezed out the straw which was essential for fodder and for fertilising the soil. The yields were 'high' from the viewpoint of centralised control of food-grain trade, but not in the context of diversity of species and products at the level of the farm and the farmer.

Overall productivity and sustainability are much higher in mixed systems of farming and forestry which produce diverse outputs. Productivity of monocultures is low in the context of diverse outputs and needs. It is high only in the restricted context of output of 'part of a part' of the forest and farm biomass. 'High yields' plantations pick one tree species among thousands, for yields of one part of the tree (eg pulpwood). 'High yield' green revolution cropping patterns pick one crop among hundreds, eg wheat for yields of one part of the wheat plant (grain only). These high partial yields do not translate into high total (including diverse) yields. Productivity is therefore different depending on whether it is measured in a framework of diversity or uniformity.

Transnational corporations (TNCs), international research systems, and multilateral agencies, which are largely run and controlled by white men who control capital, find an essential tool for control and accumulation in monocultures. Third World women, farmers and forest communities find both a means of abundance and freedom in diversity.

Intellectual Property Rights and Knowledge Monopolies

Free trade of TNCs does not translate into freedom for farmers of the Third World. TNC freedom depends on protectionist and monopoly measures like intellectual property rights (IPRs), which must rob farmers of their freedom to produce, modify and sell seeds.

However, Third World farmers are not the only community affected by IPRs in the area of biodiversity. Herbalists, forest dwellers, fishing communities, pastoralists who depend on biodiversity for their survival, and whose resources and knowledge are freely used by the TNCs which then demand IPR protection, will also be severely affected by IPRs in so-called free trade agreements.

Most discussion around Trade Related Intellectual Property Rights (TRIPs) in GATT have focused on the assumption that only the intellectual contributions of corporate-sponsored scientists need intellectual property

protection and compensation. The only North-South debate then is on how IPRs will restrict the transfer of technology from the industrialised North to the industrialising South.

However, no attention has been paid to how IPRs will encourage the uncompensated free flow of resources and knowledge from the South to the North. A very significant issue that has been missing in these debates is how the very construction of IPRs in GATT counts knowledge and innovation as only that which can generate profits. Knowledge and innovation for social ends such as health care and sustainable agriculture is discounted. The intellectual contribution of societies and communities which have not been motivated by the objective of profits is thus exploited, but not recognised. For example, ethno-botanists transfer knowledge from traditional healers to pharmaceutical firms. The intellectual property rights therefore raises multiple questions of *whose* intellect? *What* property? *Whose* rights? *What* rights?

In this wider framework, traditional farmers who have selected, improved and conserved biodiversity, or traditional healers who have used plant diversity for medicine also have prior intellectual property rights which need protection. When this knowledge and biodiversity is exploited for commercial ends, these contributors need to have a role in determining whether such exploitation should take place, and what the terms of compensation should be. IPRs in the area of biodiversity are no longer a mere matter of transfer of technology but become the ground for intercultural dialogue.

Intellectual property rights and patents in the area of life forms and living processes are an enclosure of the intellectual commons. Unlike mechanical artifacts, innovation and knowledge related to the utilisation of living resources has been a highly evolved tradition in all cultures. Innovations for which patents are being given often only build on prior knowledge and use of biological systems for food and medicine. Instead of stimulating research and knowledge generation, patents stifle creativity and communication. In the Third World where privatisation is not the norm, most knowledge generation takes place in the public domain, either in the formal or the informal sector. The formal sector includes all public sector research institutions, the informal sector includes all communities which maintain and generate knowledge related to biodiversity. IPRs as formulated in GATT will undermine knowledge generation and creativity in both these sectors.

Both the informal as well as the formal sectors are affected negatively through the intellectual enclosures engendered by patents. The informal sector innovation is destroyed by non-recognition. For example when ethno-botanists transfer knowledge from traditional healers to pharmaceutical firms, and genetic resource conservationists transfer knowledge from farmers to seed corporations, the intellectual property rights go to the corporations, not to the farmers and healers. Over time this appropriation of knowledge kills the original socio-cultural context of knowledge generation.

The formal sector of innovation and knowledge is destroyed by restricting free access to scientific knowledge due to patent restrictions. The broad patents on scientific processes, and on life forms, block the free exchange of ideas and materials, which have in the first place been taken freely from the informal sector in the biodiversity-rich Third World. Patents thus block a free flow of knowledge from the formal sector of the North to the formal sector of the South while maintaining a free flow from the informal sector of the South to the formal sector of the North. Patents also block a free flow of knowledge between the formal and informal sectors of the South since research is systematically privatised and transnationalised, breaking the vital umbilical link between science and society which is the only sustainable source for the nurture of creativity.

Biodiversity and knowledge about its utilisation, therefore, gets steadily eroded in the public domain, causing both ecological and economic impoverishment in the Third World.

TNCs see both nature and Third World farmers as a block to their market expansion. John Hamilton of Cargill India stated that Cargill's technology for making a hybrid sunflower prevents 'bees from usurping the pollen'. From the TNC perspective, even nature's freedom to reproduce life through its complex ecological webs is seen as usurpation. Similarly, small farmers freely reproducing seed are viewed as 'pirates' by those who have robbed the Third World of its biodiversity and its biological knowledge.

The TNC demand for IPRs to biodiversity is based on the false assumption that TNCs have made investments and therefore need to be rewarded with monopoly control and that their investments alone lead to innovation. These assumptions become mechanisms for robbing Third World farmers of their inalienable rights to control and reproduce seed as a means of food production. First, by treating capital investment as the only investment that must have rewards in the form of monopoly control, the centuries of investment of time and creativity by Third World farmers in domesticating, breeding and conserving biodiversity is negated.

Secondly, by recognising only corporate manipulation of life as 'improvement', improvements made by millions of Third World farmers over centuries are denied and their seed is reduced to 'raw material' to be saved in international gene banks for corporate breeding programmes.

Farmers' seeds are rendered incomplete and valueless by the process that makes corporate seeds the basis of wealth creation. The indigenous varieties or land races, evolved through both natural and human selection, and produced and used by Third World farmers worldwide are called 'primitive cultivars'. Those varieties created by modern plant breeders in international research centres or transnational seed corporations are called 'advanced' or 'elite'. The tacit hierarchy in words like 'primitive' and 'elite' becomes an explicit one in the process of conflict. Thus, the North has always used Third World germplasm as a freely available resource and treated it as valueless. The advanced capitalist nations wish to retain free access to the developing world's storehouse of genetic diversity, while 'the South' like to have the proprietary varieties of the North's industry declared a similarly 'public' good. The North, however, resists this democracy, based on the logic of the market. The corporate perspective views as value only that which serves the market. However, all material processes also serve ecological needs and social needs, and these needs are undermined by the monopolising tendency of corporations.

The issue of patent protection for modified life forms raises a number of unresolved political questions about ownership and control of genetic resources. The problem is that in manipulating life forms you do not start from nothing, but from other life forms which belong to others – maybe through customary law. Secondly, genetic engineering biotechnology does not create new genes, it merely relocates genes already existing in organisms. In making genes the object of value through the patent systems, a dangerous shift is placed in the approach to genetic resources.

Putting value on the gene through patents makes biology stand on its head. Complex organisms which have evolved over millennia in nature, and through the contributions of Third World farmers, tribespeople and healers are reduced to their parts, and these parts treated as mere inputs into genetic engineering. Patenting of genes thus leads to a devaluation of life forms by reducing them to their constituents and allowing them to be repeatedly owned as private property. This reductionism and fragmentation might be convenient for commercial concerns, but they violate the integrity of life, as well as the common property rights of Third World people. The trade wars at GATT are based on these false notions of genetic resources and their ownership through intellectual property rights. Countries like the

United States are using trade as a means of enforcing their patent laws and intellectual property rights on the sovereign nations of the Third World. The US has accused countries of the Third World of engaging in 'unfair trading practices' if they fail to adopt US patent laws which allow monopoly rights on life forms. Yet it is the US which has engaged in unfair practices related to the use of Third World genetic resources. It has freely taken the biological diversity of the Third World to spin million of dollars of profits, none of which have been shared with Third World countries, the original owners of the germplasm. A wild tomato variety (*Lycopersicon chomrelewskii*) taken from Peru in 1962 has contributed $8 million a year to the American tomato processing industry by increasing the content of soluble solids. Yet, none of these profits or benefits have been shared with Peru, the original source of the genetic material.

According to Prescott-Allen, wild varieties contributed US $340 million per year between 1976 and 1980 to the US farm economy. The total contribution of wild germplasm to the American economy has been US$66 billion, which is more than the total international debt of Mexico and the Philippines combined. This wild material is 'owned' by sovereign states and by local people.

IPRs are the central instrument of recolonisation 500 years after Columbus. Third World people who struggled for freedom from colonisation within living memory will not give up that freedom without resistance.

The seed has very rapidly become a symbol of this new struggle for freedom. The 'Seed Satyagraha' is a 'fight for truth' which attempts to tell the truth about 'free trade', using the non-violent, democratic methods of Gandhi. The question of whose freedom shall govern the future will be determined by these struggles between the corporate interest and the interest of the citizen.

A central part of the Seed Satyagraha is to declare the 'common intellectual rights' of Third World communities who have given the world the gift of their knowledge of the rich bounties of nature's diversity. The innovations of Third World communities might differ in process and objective from the innovations in the commercial world of the west. They cannot be discounted just because they are different. But we are going beyond just saying 'no'. We are creating alternatives by building community seed banks, strengthening farmers' seed supply, and searching for sustainable agriculture options suitable for particular regions.

The seed has become for us a symbol of freedom in the age of monocultures, manipulation and monopoly. It plays the role of Gandhi's spinning wheel in this period of recolonisation through free trade. The Charkha (spinning wheel) had become an important symbol of freedom, not because it was big and powerful, but because it was small and could come alive as a sign of resistance and creativity in the smallest of huts and the poorest of families. In smallness lay its power. The seed is also small. It embodies diversity. In the seed, cultural diversity converges with biological diversity. Ecological issues combine with social justice, peace and democracy.

10

THE CULTURAL DIMENSIONS OF DEVELOPMENT

Javier Pérez de Cuéllar

My endorsement of this most ambitious and comprehensive undertaking, *The Right to Hope*, is twofold:
First, as a former Secretary-General of the United Nations, I came to appreciate over the years the role intercultural communication can play in reducing the tension and misunderstanding which usually fuel racism and hatred. It can contribute significantly to the prevention, and eventually, to the peaceful resolution of conflicts around the world. This is true in the diplomatic field or any other field for that matter – at the national as well as on the global scale.

Furthermore, I personally believe that democratic dialogue and exchanges of opinion on an equal footing are at the root of harmonious political, social and economic relations within countries themselves, not to mention between nations.

The second is in my present capacity as President of the World Commission on Culture and Development (WCCD), which was established precisely because the development models based solely on economic growth are showing their limits. Indeed, after three decades dedicated to the exclusive search for material gain it became obvious that, far from diminishing, the gap between the wealthiest and poorest countries had widened. Moreover, inside the countries themselves, both in the North and the South, the gulf keeps expanding between a minority who has access to education and well-being and a large majority of people who are excluded.

This trend has to be slowed, then ultimately stopped and reversed. This is why UNESCO and the United Nations established, at the end of 1992, our independent Commission, composed of leading figures, including four Nobel Prize winners, such as Elie Wiesel and Ms Aung San Suu Kyi. Its main objective is to explore – for the first time ever at the global level – the ties that bind culture and development, and to prepare a World Report on the subject by the end of 1995.

We are convinced that, like peace and democracy, development cannot be reduced to economic growth alone, that development has its roots in culture. Culture, in our view, is not merely an abstract notion accessible to a chosen few. On the contrary, culture is what we really are, it shapes our behaviour, our vision of the world. As a result, any development effort which is not founded on the respect for different cultures, for their equal dignity and their diversity, is doomed to fail.

This is an important reminder at a time when collective technological and scientific advances tend to capture all our attention at the expense of our cultural roots and identity; at a time when indigenous cultures are being scorned, if not all together disregarded, as merely 'traditional' or outdated in favour of imported models ignorant of their genuine needs; at a time when, as a result, our civilisation – or should I say civilisations – undergo an acute crisis in which the

role of individuals is being questioned and the lack of vision for their futures deplored.

Since the beginning of time, artists have been the critics and the prophets of civilisation. It is therefore only natural that their work is highlighted today as a driving force of different cultural perceptions of the same complex world.

That is why a new type of development – human, sustainable and shared – is called for; a development of the people, by the people and for the people. A development that takes into account the cultural specifics of the individual and each community. In short, a development based on culture.

How would this new concept affect our everyday life? By making the cities, once again, a place where people can live, enjoy themselves and benefit culturally from each other's experiences; by promoting cultural tourism, respectful of local traditions, as a source of dialogue and exchanges between people; by expanding the role of amateur cultural and artistic practices, so exercising our innate creativity; in short, by paying attention to the cultural specifics and diversity in the development process.

This book contributes precisely to making that point. It shows how initiative and inspiration in the field of culture and development can sometimes come from the grass-roots level up, and not the other way round. Its goal, which is to demonstrate that despite our natural differences and diversity we belong to the same world we seek to improve together for the generations to come, can therefore only be endorsed by the Commission I have the honour to chair.

The establishment of our independent Commission is to be seen in the context of the World Decade for Cultural Development. This Decade, which is being celebrated under the joint auspices of the United Nations and UNESCO, should be leading to a recharging, and I might even say to a conversion, of policies. It should put the cultural dimension at the heart of that other, human, sustainable and shared form of development.

If we do not wish to go backwards into the third millennium, we have to rethink development. We have to rethink the very notion of culture. Since it has never been done on a world scale, we must go more deeply into the links between culture and development. Above all, we must put forward new solutions and illuminate the way to action.

In its original sense, development signifies unfolding, extension, expansion and projection beyond the cycle of work and days. Development means becoming something from what one is – it means becoming what one actually is. In other words, development cannot be reduced just to an increase in material resources. More than ever, it needs 'more of the soul'. Quite clearly, for those who have nothing, the prime objective is to fulfil their needs but for everyone surely, the aim is henceforth to *live better* and to live better *together*. We must therefore opt for quality and pin our hopes on sharing and solidarity.

I think that the international community should set itself a common aim, namely, as the 21st century approaches, to launch a world initiative for sustainable growth, which could be firmly established only on the basis of cultural development.

A step towards this aim requires a call for a reduction in unproductive expenditure, particularly military expenditure, in all countries. This implies a search for optimisation in public expenditure and requires new pricing policies that will take account of non-economic, environmental and cultural costs. It implies the need for new fiscal policies, new commercial policies, and for the allocation of greater resources to human and cultural development – especially through education – and finally, for official development assistance and a better allocation of such assistance.

The time has surely come when all those industrialised countries that provide official development assistance and that have neither exceeded nor achieved the objective jointly prescribed by the international community – at the Rio Summit of 1992 – of giving 0.7 per cent of their gross national product for international solidarity, should at last do so.

Combating ignorance, indolence and poverty is, of course, the first priority. The *Human Development Report* stresses

that almost 83 per cent of the world's income is today in the hands of the wealthiest 20 per cent of the population. For the 20 per cent of the poorest population, there remains 1.4 per cent of the world's income. In the 1960s the share of the richest population was 70 per cent and that of the poorest 2.3 per cent. An abyss of this kind cannot be filled and the exclusion which, in North and South alike, is dividing our societies into two cannot be overcome just by injecting capital, infrastructure, technology or expertise. Ready-made, turnkey happiness has been a failure. Today, as UNDP emphasises, less than 10 per cent of the world's population plays a full part in political, economic, social and cultural life.

Our Commission will elaborate policy recommendations with a view to promoting genuine commitment to cultural pluralism; greater recognition of the place of cultural diversity in development; and the key role of creativity as a lever of development and the development potential of the new media technologies. We are convinced that far from being a mere legacy, culture, today under threat, is the only horizon we have in common. We can no longer ignore it: our patterns of development based on the continuous expansion of material consumption are neither viable nor infinitely extensible. They not only tear the fabric of cultures but they threaten the biosphere and hence the survival of humanity.

The transition to sustainable development implies a radical change in the styles of development in North and South alike. It cannot succeed unless new patterns of development and new cultural policies come to the fore that follow plural trajectories, do not endanger bio-diversity, are rooted in cultural diversity and are based on the achievements of science and modern technology. In future, development patterns must therefore be focused on *people* and foster the development of cultural values instead of harming them. Where both the natural and the cultural environments are concerned, the problem today is not so much one of establishing control as of setting limits to it.

The conclusion of a genuine social and moral contract and even of the 'natural contract' outlined at Rio calls for a new pact among human beings – a cultural contract. This is because any development which does not draw its strength from the rich potential of memory, creativity and innovation that culture has to offer is liable to fail or be short-lived and to jeopardise the diversity and vitality of cultures, which derive their sustenance from exchange and dialogue. What is more, the alternative form of development to which we aspire should lead to a growth in the resources, opportunities and scope for action offered to all individuals and all groups. It will not be able to generate new models that are relevant to both global and local realities unless, both upstream and downstream from policies, there is a profound change in attitudes and lifestyles – and this requires full-scale cultural transformations.

If we really want to prepare for the 21st century, if we want to give a chance to the kind of sustainable human development based on solidarity to which I have referred, we shall have to change our behaviour radically, and change it soon. We are going to have to re-create a common fund of shared values, paying due regard to our separate identities.

Some will say that this is a pipe-dream. My answer to them is that the most important social and historical transformation of our time, along with decolonialisation, has undoubtedly been the change in the situation of women and their role in society. Nevertheless, this cultural revolution, which is nowhere near completion, was not in the manifestos of any of the political parties. It has forced itself upon them. This upheaval has come about collectively, anonymously and in the course of everyday life. It has been and will be brought about by women themselves and this is also true of the current demographic transition.

The cards of the 21st century are being shuffled before our eyes; suffice it to mention the scientific and technological revolution, the eruption of the worldwide communication society, the globalisation of the world economy, the political upheavals and the cross-currents of global integration and national disintegration. Our universe is fraught with perils and uncertainties, yet rich in new potential.

A bridge must be built between the visionary and the decision-maker, between seeing and foreseeing, between creators and economists. This will enable us to lay the foundations of an Agenda for Culture and Development that will be complementary to the Brundtland Report and Agenda 21. Such an Agenda will comprise not only a concrete, programmatic and practical plan of action but will also reform proposals and recommendations on arrangements for follow-up, financing and implementation.

As André Malraux said, the world of culture 'is not one of immortality; it is one of metamorphosis'. Far from being an obstacle to modernisation, culture is the key to development and its horizon – since development encompasses all the wealth of human experience. Emerson once said: 'Hitch your wagon to a star'. What better symbol could there be? If culture becomes the lodestar of development, if it becomes one of the top priorities on national and international agendas, we shall have preserved the only part of our human heritage that is as yet unspoiled – the virgin lands of the future.

11

Governance in our Global Neighbourhood

Shridath Ramphal

What the artist with his distinctive antennae is quick to sense – that the world is one and the divisions that separate nations are artificial – the astronaut and the space camera were able to confirm. The poet Archibald McLeish put the message from the 1968 Apollo space mission into words most eloquently:

> *To see the earth as we now see it, small and blue and beautiful in that eternal silence where it floats, is to see ourselves as riders on the earth together, brothers on that bright loveliness in the unending night – brothers who see now they are truly brothers.*

Global governance – our arrangements for the conduct of our common affairs – must respect the moral imperatives of that message, which is articulated today in numerous ways in the gathering evidence of human interdependence. Few developments have done so more convincingly than the increasing damage caused to the environment, which sustains life on earth and whose degradation makes all vulnerable.

The wider recognition of our common humanity is also underlined by the great movements of our time, all transnational in their sweep: movements to protect human rights, to fight poverty, to empower women, to end apartheid, to outlaw nuclear weapons, to green the planet.

In many ways the frontiers between nation states, whether sea or land, are becoming more penetrable and therefore less relevant and made to look artificial. Border controls may still shut out people but not ideas and images. These are less easy to intercept and move much more freely and so more widely, thanks to recent leaps in satellite, computer and communications technology.

Even more important to our sense of being one world is the increasing need to join hands across national boundaries and work together. A thickening web of interdependence enmeshes humanity, requiring nations to share efforts whether it is to maintain peace and order, expand economic activity, avoid global warming, preserve natural resources, combat drug rings, terrorists or criminal syndicates, control the spread of weapons, fight killer diseases or save threatened species.

We are more and more affected by what happens elsewhere, even far away. An economic slowdown in the United States, a crop failure in Russia or unrest in North Africa can have repercussions far afield. A booming East Asia can protect jobs in North America. European tariff cuts can cause fewer trees to be felled in the tropics. Lower greenhouse gas emissions in industrial countries may save islands in the Maldives from being submerged by rising sea levels. Reduced CFC use in Europe will lead to fewer cases of skin cancer in South America.

These are all intimations of the world's oneness. They are also evidence of how small the world has become. Technology has overcome distance and made remoteness rare. More people travel longer, faster. Words and pictures

travel even quicker, far quicker. These changes have transformed the world – into a neighbourhood.

We are now citizens of the global neighbourhood. We must live by neighbourhood values, being good neighbours to one another, sharing our endowment, accepting our responsibilities for promoting the common welfare even as we protect our rights and entitlements.

Governance must today adjust its focus to put people at the centre. Nation-states will continue to be the chief players in the global system, but the interests of people must not be subordinated to those of states. Those who hold power within states must not be free to shelter behind the shield of state sovereignty when they trample on the rights of their people.

Our institutions of governance and their procedures have to be reformed to take account of these needs. And some tenets of the international system, such as the principle that states should not intervene in the internal affairs of other sovereign states, have to be adapted so that the rights of people may not be sacrificed at the altar of state sovereignty. If, for instance, the security of people within a country is massively endangered, whether by the actions of a tyrannical ruler, the collapse of civil order, or even a natural disaster, the international community of states should have the right to intervene to protect those people.

International law, in this case the Charter of the United Nations, permits intervention only when international peace is at risk. The UN Security Council has occasionally stretched this rule to authorise intervention in internal situations. But it is far better to change the rules to make intervention legitimate under prescribed conditions. That would offer protection to people but, while allowing intervention, would also place limits on it to guard against arbitrary or unprincipled action.

Such a change would give more power to the Security Council. That makes it all the more necessary that the Council should itself be reformed to make it more representative. It is the world's most powerful body, and power has resided with the same five countries – the five Permanent Members – since it was set up in 1945. Then there were only 51 countries in the UN and now there are 186. The 'big five' have so far agreed to only one, modest change: to raise the number of rotating or non-permanent members, who serve for only two years at a time, from six to ten, and that was 30 years ago.

The Commission on Global Governance, which issued its report *The Global Neighbourhood* in January 1995, called for a two-stage reform of the Council, leading to the abolition of permanent members and their right to veto Council decisions. As a first step it proposed a new class of 'standing' members who would serve longer than non-permanent members; it suggested that two industrial countries, one Asian and the other European, and three developing countries, one each from Asia, Africa and Latin America, should be the first 'standing' members. The Commission also called for three more rotating members, so that the Council would be enlarged to twenty-three.

In the Commission, we saw the need to widen the definition of security so that international governance protects people not only against violence in the form of interstate aggression and war but also against other forms of insecurity. On a day-to-day basis, economic insecurity, whether it is the lack of a livelihood in a poor country or the loss of employment in a rich country, blights more lives than the risk of military conflict. The persistence of acute deprivation and the continuing increase in the number of the absolute poor in the developing world are hard realities though they tend to be overshadowed by the dramatic performance of the East Asian tigers, who are now being followed by a second wave of much more populous countries, including China. There are now also fears of an underclass becoming an endemic feature in many industrially advanced societies, which have also been scarred by abnormally high unemployment.

The need to give a greater impetus – and a higher profile – to efforts to improve economic security for people worldwide led the Commission to call for an Economic Security Council as an apex body within the United Nations to give policy leadership on economic and related issues. The only high-level economic co-ordination now attempted is by the Group of Seven (G7) industrial countries. Besides being self-appointed, this group represents only industrial countries, and it does not even constitute the world's seven largest economies. When countries' Gross Domestic Product is measured not using prevailing exchange rates but taking into account what money can actually buy in each country – what economists call 'purchasing power parities' – China is the world's third largest economy, after the US and Japan, and India the fifth, after Germany. But China and India have no place in the G7; Britain and Canada, which are in the G7, are eighth and thirteenth in the world rankings.

More effective and equitable governance responding to the needs of the world as a whole calls for an economic forum that is more representative than the G7 and is mindful of the interests of all nations, both industrial and developing. In view of the nature of issues it would deal with, it would not be appropriate for it to be a decision-making body like the Security Council. It should be a deliberative organ whose stature ensures that its views influence the conduct of key international institutions, such as the International Monetary Fund and the World Bank, as well as of regional bodies and national governments.

The shared interests of the world's people would also be better served by new arrangements for governance of the global commons: the atmosphere, outer space, the oceans beyond the areas under national control, and the related environment and life-support systems that help to sustain human life. Prudent management of the global commons, including development and controlled use of their resources and prevention of overuse, could be crucial to planetary security and the future well-being, perhaps even survival, of humanity. This management is best overseen by a body acting on behalf of all nations, because the commons belong to them all. We have suggested that the UN Trusteeship Council, which has shepherded all its trust territories to self-government or independence, should now be reconstituted as trustees of the global commons, on behalf of the present and future generations.

Another thrust of the recommendations made by the Commission is in the direction of involving people more closely in global governance. This complements the sharper focus on people and their interests in international arrangements for security in its widest dimensions. One specific proposal is for a new forum of representatives of civil society to be set up to meet each year at the United Nations in New York and make a contribution to the annual sessions of the UN General Assembly on behalf of the people of the world. Another proposal envisages people's organisations having direct access to a new UN Council for Petitions so that they may trigger international consideration of situations that could lead to extensive violations of people's security in any country.

The past five decades have transformed the world in many ways but the world's governance has yet to adapt fully to respond to, and take advantage of, the new circumstances. Although the word 'spiritual' is rarely used in the corridors of the United Nations, it is increasingly accepted that the future of the organization depends upon the development of universal values in the minds and hearts of the peoples of the world – a point powerfully made by the Commission.

Freed of the obsessive rivalries and corrosive tensions of the Cold War, the world has an opportunity to build a more just, more secure, more democratic order for its people. The fiftieth anniversary of the United Nations should spur us to transcend our differences and strengthen our resolve to work together to make the world we share a better world for all humankind – a better global neighbourhood.

12

THE GLOBAL AND THE LOCAL: PLANTING SEEDS OF HOPE

Alicia Barcena

THE NEW GLOBAL REALITIES

The fall of the Berlin Wall, one of the most resonant myths of our century, marked the end of a long Cold War period, artificially maintained by two blocks of nations headed by the Soviet Union and the United States. Although the threat of a thermonuclear Third World War never materialised, the period was characterised by a permanent ideological, commercial and military confrontation plagued by microwars and regional, national and ethnic conflicts for which the international community was not prepared.

At the end of the millennium, the whole world is going through an extraordinary and unprecedented process of change in the quest for a new international order. However, the ideal of an equitable order or development model has been displaced in the last few years by a reality dominated by monetarism, militarism (both local and transnational), and media-driven consumerism, creating a severe crisis of values at the individual, family and social level.

The spectre of runaway globalisation, which a majority of the world population finds difficult to understand, threatens to perpetuate social and economic inequities under the ideological blanket of free markets, competitiveness, consumerism, productivism, and short-term technological efficiency, all of which lead to a severe decrease in the quality of life and an unsustainable loss of natural resources. A unipolar world characterised by the ideological and cultural domination of free-market capitalism.

This economic paradigm is leading to a world fragmented into two: that of the included, and that of the excluded. The included are those countries that have managed to join an economic system based on access to capital, technology and information. This dementedly high mobility of capital and the inadequate transference of technology and information are leading to an unprecedented crisis that is out of the control of international organisations like the IMF or the Group of Seven.

In recent years, we have gone from a world divided into two ideological camps, socialism and capitalism, to one ideologically unified by the belief in free markets but separated by a growing economic and social gap between rich and poor, both at the global and national levels. This reality of two worlds underscores the increasing urgency to search for alternative development models, a new ethic, and respect for the many possible new approaches based on the cultural and natural diversity and social rhythms of each community. We are at a crossroads leading, on the one hand, to more homogeneity and, on the other, to the opportunity to find a kaleidoscope of local answers.

The current development model has emphasised economic growth and the concentration of wealth based on the exploitation of national and foreign natural resources through monetary pressures, the transformations wrought by

technology, and the monopolisation of the world media. Rich countries have devised a palliative scheme: it is what is called overseas development aid (ODA), channelled through the agencies of the United Nations and some programmes of the World Bank, regional development banks, bilateral agreements, and so on.

The current situation of international cooperation is dire and worrisome, both in terms of numbers and goals; it is conditioned more by ideology than by any real programme to promote development. The daily flow of private capital in the world market is close to $3 trillion, while the annual amount spent in development aid by OECD countries to developing nations is approximately $65 billion (1992 figures). Moreover, economic assistance by NGOs in the North to their counterparts in the South is not much higher than $9 billion. ODA spending is equivalent to less than 0.3 per cent of the gross national product of industrialised nations, and this amount, instead of growing, has fallen by approximately 10 per cent in the last two years, since much of the aid has been dedicated to humanitarian assistance, especially in Africa, and not to real development programmes.

The decline in development assistance has been accompanied by a tendency towards bilateralism, regionalism and the promotion of regional trade blocks, posing a serious threat to horizontal, multilateral cooperation. The map of geopolitical alliances has been replaced by one of economic and free-trade unions fostered by the Bretton Woods institutions (the International Monetary Fund, the World Bank and the World Trade Organisation), the main promoters of free trade, structural adjustment, and leaner government structures. This global situation is weakening everything that is public, governmental and collective.

Capital, knowledge and technology are escaping from the hands of States. They are being privatised and transnationalised. The globalisation of financial markets, without a world authority to supervise and regulate them, is threatening the stability of the world economy. Structural adjustment programmes, in tandem with external free-trade pressures, have weakened severely the social and economic capacity of developing countries. National initiatives have been crushed by the emphasis on foreign investment. Everything has been adapted to facilitate the transnationalisation of economies. Such global conditions have weakened the delicate economic, cultural and social fabric at the regional, national and local level. Indeed, speculative activities may lead to a generalised world financial collapse.

One of the sectors most affected by this process is that of food production. It is a national security issue which has been globalised. Today, many countries solve the question of how to feed their populations by means of costly imports, leading to the displacement of the rural population in search of that modern mirage: urban prosperity. Loss of control of their own processes has generated a model of dependent consumerism, the goal of which is to concentrate people in cities with less expensive infrastructure and services; there, human beings produce in order to consume. Every action carried out in this context is an act of trade, of consumption, allowing intermediaries to proliferate and weakening the connection between humanity and nature. The planet's metabolism is being accelerated to satisfy monetary policies and the consumerism of the few, at the cost of limiting the options of millions now and in the future.

Developing nations have been subjected to strong modernising and privatising pressures, together with growing foreign debt, increasing social and political deterioration, a very limited savings capacity and the establishment of financial markets which facilitate the high volatility of capital. All this has taken place at the cost of mortgaging the future. Natural resources, human well-being, and the future have been devalued.

In the last 20 years, the various actors have played their part in a process no one yet understands. Politicians feel obliged to provide short-term answers, with a growing loss of real power and capacity to manoeuvre. The national private sector feels like the great winner of the capitalist model, and yet faces the daunting rivalry of transnational corporations, setting the stage for an unprecedented conflict between small and medium-sized local and national producers and their multinational competitors.

The IMF has failed in its mission to regulate international monetary and macroeconomic policies, by concentrating its influence exclusively on developing countries and becoming an instrument for privatisation and for loans conditioned on structural adjustment policies which wreak social and political havoc and increasingly weaken the role of the State.

Even as, in theory, developing countries are becoming more democratic, governments and States are moving further and further away from the grassroots; by protecting and supporting international economic interests in the quest for modernisation and foreign investment, they have neglected their own national and public interests and their own small-scale producers. In developing nations, this has led to the devaluation of natural and human resources and to growing financial conflicts. These circumstances have generated a crisis of governance easily seen in the distrust that ordinary citizens feel for their governments. In many cases, this has produced the conditions for the growth of non-governmental organisations (NGOs) as a new form of civil pressure.

The generalised growth of NGOs has been manipulated at times by the powerful to generate the illusion of participatory processes, while leaving out the real social actors of development. This suggests the need to review carefully the sociology of the non-governmental sector, and to evaluate the role, the representativeness, and the contribution of each actor to the process of building a new development model. Governments are therefore not the only actors that will define the course humanity will take: there are many other important influences, particularly NGOs, the media and transnational corporations.

It was in this international atmosphere of change that the United Nations Conference on Environment and Development (UNCED), or Earth Summit, was held in Rio de Janeiro in June 1992, the culmination of over two years of negotiations by 182 countries. The Earth Summit was an important historical landmark. First, it was characterised by an unprecedented level of involvement by civil, religious, academic, environmental and development organisations. In addition, it was the first time that the twin issues of environment and development were discussed in a cross-sectoral, and not just sectoral, fashion.

Since the mid-1980s, the concept of sustainable development has emerged as an attempt to bring together the various strands of an alternative development model that would include social justice, the environmental conservation of the planet, the search for a new economic paradigm, and a new participatory democracy in lieu of the representative democracies that simply conceal the basically authoritarian nature of free-trade economics.

UNCED provided a unique opportunity to reflect on the global trends mentioned above and their connection with the development policies of recent decades. It turned into a forum where ideologies were examined and confronted; and one where, during the negotiations, the traditional regional groups were replaced in practice by the new regional free-trade blocks. During the two years of preparatory meetings for the Conference, innovative ways were found for achieving international consensus and allowing the participation of non-governmental actors. The Conference was without precedent in its achievement of agreements and action programmes that point the way to a new form of international cooperation in the fields of environment and development.

At the Earth Summit, it became apparent that the human species is at a crossroads, where the opportunities are great, but so are the dangers of failure. The current economic model has produced material wealth and a technological revolution without precedent, but it has also been characterised by the way it favours a minority. Developed nations have based their economic growth on the impoverishment of other countries. Such a model is not sustainable, as it has led to a dangerous instability that now threatens the whole of humanity.

There were five main outcomes of the Conference:

1. The Rio Declaration on Environment and Development, a political document listing 27 principles that should guide the behaviour of nations and peoples to ensure the viability of the planet as a safe and equitable home for human beings;

2. Agenda 21, the first global action plan negotiated by governments and arrived at by consensus that breaks down the concept of sustainable development into intersectoral and multi-participatory actions and commitments;

3. The Convention on Biological Diversity, a legal instrument aimed at regulating international and national actions concerning renewable natural resources, their ownership, protection, value and commercial use;

4. The Framework Convention of the United Nations on Climate Change, a legal instrument aimed at promoting a transition to more sustainable energy and industry practices that will protect the atmosphere as a collective good essential to life; and

5. The Principles for a World Consensus on the Use, Conservation and Development of Forests of all Kinds.

Three years after the Summit, many consider it a failure for not having achieved the necessary change of economic paradigm to make sustainable development possible. Instead, the Bretton Woods institutions, with their classical models of free markets and structural adjustments, have been strengthened. Nevertheless, it is important to see the Summit and its results as a starting point and as a rallying cry. The most astonishing conclusion that can be drawn from the Summit and its aftermath is that the change of paradigms and structures will not come from governments, but from the actions and pressures of non-governmental actors. The most valuable lesson of Rio was that it is the countries of the South who can show the world a model of sustainable development, because most of them have the necessary moral, ethical and cultural values.

Planting Seeds of Hope: the Local is Viable

The unstable economic equilibrium achieved in some parts of the globe, and the certainty that the neoclassical economic approach does not provide an appropriate conceptual framework for development, has led many social actors to push for change. Regrettably, this has led to a growing militarisation, and political systems are becoming more authoritarian and technocratic.

It is imperative for humanity to find ways to leave behind environmental degradation and an economic system in which growth can only be achieved at the cost of massive impoverishment, and move towards a new, dynamic equilibrium that revitalises the social and environmental, and can build a new economic paradigm. The social justice demanded by developing countries consists simply in everyone having enough, without having too much, and in building the kinds of communities that allow all of their members to benefit from nature's bounty in such a way that they can live well without putting the future at risk.

The main challenge we face is to devise new approaches based on the convergence of three goals: economic growth, social equity and environmental sustainability. The many interpretations of the concept of sustainable development show the urgent need for the various actors of development to search for consensus on its implementation in accordance with local conditions.

The democratisation of capital, information and education, and the strengthening and legitimising of participatory decision-making mechanisms are essential elements of these new approaches. A new social contract is required in which governments and non-governmental actors, in the widest possible sense of the word, can decide what their own project is for their country and for their community. In this process, one basic condition is the building of consensus to allow all actors to overcome the most critical obstacle to national and local development: the high cost of capital and technology, and limited access to information.

The process should begin at the local community level on the basis of these premises: that family groups (rather than corporate firms) are the basic unit of production, and that the local communities made up of these family groups could be seen as enterprises in a capitalist system that is community-based, along similar lines to the worker-shareholder schemes currently being implemented in the United States and Europe. Such community enterprises should be designed bearing in mind the local ecosystem, its unique economic characteristics, its natural resources and biodiversity, its sustainable use, and so on. This model is based on local equity rather than on macroeconomic models that propose a so-far unsuccessful trickle-down effect. All this entails abandoning centralist policies and replacing them with local governance systems based on an awareness of the local geographical, ecological and cultural realities. The exchange of commodities and finished products must again take place at the local level, creating an economic circle in which communities can again control their own social, ecological and economic processes.

Consumption and production patterns must get back to the virtues of traditional knowledge, which may be supported by modern technology, but not the other way around, since the indiscriminate use of new technologies changes the productive and cultural traditions that communities apply in their interaction with nature. This alternative approach is not a call for a return to neolithic times. On the contrary, it seeks to overcome the way of thinking that divides people into conquerors and the conquered. It would encourage the adaptation of the most modern technologies, but would reject the manipulation of the community's economic activities by the State and foreign trade agents. The goal is to strengthen community activities based on diversified production methods conceived from the point of view of the final beneficiaries: family groups and ecosystems.

The seeds of hope for our planet reside in the potential of our peoples to build this new world order. What is required is the creation of a new concept of local sovereignty in which the property of natural, social and cultural wealth remains in the hands of the communities where this wealth is generated. It is not a question of rejecting all external influences, but of accepting them on a case-by-case basis if they are in agreement with the community's own plans for itself, enabling it to graft modernity and global priorities onto local conditions and the goals, values and cultural heritage of each community.

We need to find ways of revitalising the skills of our local communities – building consensus, administering their own affairs in a participatory manner, placing a high worth on their local resources, relying on their own values – and thus build a set of community-based indicators of sustainable development. Such is the most important challenge posed to our generation: the creation of our equitable, common future.

13

*V*ISIONS FOR THE *F*UTURE

Phil Lane

With the heartfelt understanding that each one of us is the spiritual representative of all those beloved relatives who have gone before us, I have complete faith that we will be able to build a new world civilisation. Drawing on this collective consciousness of countless previous generations, we have the divine capacity to resolve and heal all past grief and hatred while building a new world that will fully realise the vast potential of the human family, both individually and collectively.

We are living in the days of the fulfilment of ancient sacred prophecies. An Elder once told me, 'Grandson, the longest road you will ever have to walk in your life is the sacred journey from your head to your heart.' Another wise Elder said, 'We will never solve the many critical and life threatening issues before us solely through the intellect; for every problem the intellect solves it creates ten more.' Unto itself the intellect is a sacred gift of the Creator but without an open, visionary and creative heart there is no wisdom. Both the mind and heart are sacred. Both are inseparably connected. Countless centuries ago, our ancient tribal prophecies clearly spoke of the day that is now unfolding before us. It is towards the vision of establishing a new world civilization founded in spiritual principles and values that I wish to speak to you, to share with you the innermost feelings and thoughts of my heart and mind.

In December 1982, on the high plains of Alberta, forty wise, respected and dedicated elders, spiritual leaders and community members from different tribal societies across North America came together for four days and nights of consultation. Our common purpose was to derive a model of human and community development, inspired and guided by organising principles, values, strategies and processes of sustainable change and healing rooted deep in the natural laws that are at the innermost core of tribal cultures throughout Mother Earth. During this ongoing consultation, sixteen principles emerged which embody the spiritual guidance, understanding, wisdom, strength, vision and faith needed for our healing journey. It also became very clear to us that as we heal ourselves and our communties, tribal peoples will have a greater and greater role to play in the positive unfolding of a new world.

Before outlining these key guiding principles, we should perhaps ask what are the most pressing challenges before us that must be addressed if we are to survive as noble, just, compassionate, truthful and forgiving human beings and societies?

1. Environmental destruction is increasing throughout our planet. Along with that destruction, indigenous populations are rapidly disappearing. Unless there is a dramatic change in our actions towards our sacred Mother Earth, humanity's ultimate survival is more than doubtful. During the early years of America's 'new' ecological consciousness, my grandfather had a conversation with an old friend while visiting the Standing Rock Sioux Reservation in South Dakota . He asked my grandfather to explain to him what ecology was all about. 'Well' my grandfather said, 'you know we have educational institutions where you can go to study books, and talk and learn

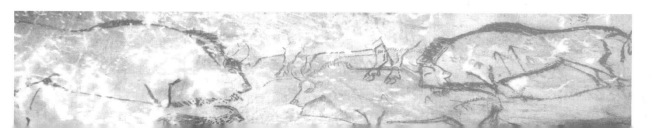

about life. Some people attend these institutions for many, many years. After they have read enough books, written about what they've read, and talked about what they've written about, they become doctors of life. These doctors then get jobs where they earn a lot of money, so they can talk and study more. They have machines that look at things that are real small and make them look big, and other machines that look at things far away and make them look close. They even put different materials in containers and pour them back and forth so they can find out more about Mother Earth. Anyway, they've spent great amounts of money and studied Mother Earth for many, many years and they've recently made a new discovery. They found out that everything is interrelated. They found out that when your pollute the air which all living things breathe and pollute the water which all living things drink, you pollute all living things.'

The old man smiled knowingly and shook his head. 'I was wondering when they would get around to that! Just look at what we do to our Mother Earth. We cut her hair where is should not be cut and rip up her skin where it should not be ripped up. Then we drill holes inside her and suck all of her blood out and put things inside of her and blow her bones up.' He looked deeply into my grandfather's eyes and shook his finger. 'And what would happen if you did that to your mother? She would die! And this is exectly what is going to happen to all of us if we don't learn to respect and understand the spirit and teachings of our sacred Mother.'

2. The world's population is increasing by more than 92,000,000 people every year. In fact, if every human being who now lives on earth were able to experience the average economic status found in middle income homes in North America, we would need two more entire planets. Until we thoroughly understand the true meaning of respect for all life, and the sacredness of the relationship between woman and man, we will continue to move towards worldwide disaster.

3. Global economic competition is increasing. The current economic system is completely out of control despite the best efforts of our nation states. Instead of sovereignty in its truest sense, financial institutions of this world are unwisely attempting to manipulate and control our economic and social destiny for selfish purposes. For instance, the stock markets of the world are increasingly destabilised by financial speculators whose primary motive appears to be the unquenchable thirst for material riches at whatever the cost to future generations. More economic theories and external controls will not solve this ever-deepening crisis. Only when we all understand that the fundamental solution to our economic problems is spiritual will we ever eliminate the tyranny of the extremes of wealth and poverty. Only when our hearts experience the divine reality that there is only one race, the human race, and that all of Mother Earth is the common spiritual heritage of all beings, will we be able to develop economic systems that are life preserving and life sustaining. As a wise Elder once told me, whenever we make economic gain on the weakness of others or unfairly exploit others for our own selfish purposes, we will pay a very high price. In essence, the hurt of one is the hurt of all, and the honour of one is the honour of all.

4. The social and cultural disintegration of human beings and their communities is increasing with every passing hour. Divorce, child sexual abuse, teenage pregnancy, substance abuse, family violence, abuse of women, violent crimes, suicide and other clear signs of our ever increasing human sickness is as clear to see as the midday sun. Only when we are able to understand and embrace one another as sisters and brothers will we have an everlasting foundation for rebuilding our communities and the world.

As one of my grandfathers said to me, 'You know, grandson, the Great Spirit, Wakan Tanka, has given all people wisdom. To every living thing he has given something special. Some people receive their knowledge and

understanding through books. In your life grandson, you too must read and study books, but remember to take with you on your journey only those things that bring more unity within yourself and others, that bring goodness and understanding and help us to serve one another in better ways. Wakan Tanka also gave our native people, and all other people who live close to Mother Earth, wisdom and knowledge through dreams, visions, fasting, prayer, and the ability to see the lessons the Creator has put in every part of the world around us. Look at those trees standing over there; the alder does not tell the pine tree to move over; the pine does not tell the fir tree to move over; each tree stands there in unity, with their mouth pressed toward the same Mother Earth, refreshed by the same breeze, warmed by the same sun, with their arms raised in prayer and thanksgiving, protecting one another. If we are to have peace in the world, we too must learn to live like those trees. Look, grandson, at the beautiful teachings the Creator has put in the little stream. Feel the water and see how gently and lovingly it touches your hands. It travels through deserts and mountains and many places, but it never turns its back on anyone or anything. Even though it gives life to all living things, it is very humble, for it always seeks the very lowest spot. But it has great faith, power and patience for even if a mountain stands in its path, it keeps moving and moving until finally that mountain is washed into the sea and is no more. These are the spiritual gifts that the Creator has given each one of us and if we are to be happy within ourselves and with one another, we too must develop these gifts.'

5. As the old world order becomes increasingly unstable, human rights violations are increasing everywhere. As these abuses increase, an ever greater number of people will react to them with greater violence; acts of violence not only against governments but beween ethnic and racial groups as well. The spiritual reality, at this point in history and present world framework, is that the old world order is no longer able to meet the needs of all the peoples on earth. Only by providing positive alternatives to the destruction and unharmonious patterns of living will we be able to rebuild our families and communities. Without love and forgiveness for ourselves and others we will be unable to heal the age old fear, mistrust, greed, selfishness and hatred that is destroying the heart of the human family. External control and repression of the human spirit will not end the devastation of our worldwide social order. Only self-discipline and vision in the service of the Creator, ourselves and others will enable us to be victorious over all the abuse of the human spirit that surrounds every human being.

6. As governments become more rigid, abusive and uncompromising in a last ditch effort to save the disintegrating institutions of the old world order, terrorism and random acts of violence will increase dramatically. This movement of disintegration will continue until the ancient teachings found at the heart of all living cultures and spiritual traditions are once again alive. We have a critical decision before us. Will we continue to walk the path of hatred and revenge or will we choose to walk the path of healing? Each have their clear consequences. I believe we will take the sacred path of healing, the path foretold in our ancient prophecies, as the spiritual greatness of our tribal peoples is returning with greater and greater strength.

Not only is each one of these challenges monumental in themselves, but we are approaching global catastrophe as the crossroads at which they all meet is coming rapidly into view. It will take bold and selfless action to avert such destruction; the choice to do so is ours, and that decision is ultimately a spiritual one.

The Principles for a Sustainable Society

The following sixteen principles for building a sustainable world emerged from a twelve year process of reflection, consultation and action within tribal communities across North America. They are rooted in the concerns of hundreds of aboriginal elders and leaders, as well as in the best thinking of many non-aboriginal scholars, researchers and human and community development practitioners. These principles describe the way we must work together, and what we must protect and cherish. We offer them as a gift to all those who seek to build a sustainable world, and as a foundation for a worldwide consultation process.

- *Development comes from within*
  The process of healing and development unfolds from within each person, relationship, family, community and nation.

- *Vision*
  A vision of who we can become is like a magnet drawing us to our potential. Where there is no vision, there can be no development.

- *Culturally based*
  Healing and development must be rooted in the wisdom, knowledge and living processes of our cultures.

- *Interconnectedness*
  Because everything is connected to everything else, any aspect of our healing and development is related to all the others – personal, social, political, economic. When we work on any part, the whole circle is affected.

- *Working in a circle*
  Personal healing and growth, and the healing and development of our families and communities must go hand in hand. Working on one level without attending to the other is not enough. Personal and social development as well as top-down and bottom-up approaches must be balanced.

- *Unity*
  We need the love, support and caring of others to heal and develop ourselves. Unity is the starting point and as development unfolds, unity deepens.

- *Participation*
  People have to be actively engaged in the process of their own healing and development. Without participation, there can be no development.

- *Justice*
  Every person must be treated with respect as a being and child of the Creator, regardless of gender, race, culture, religion or any other reason. Everyone should be accorded the opportunity to fully participate in the process of healing and development, and to receive a share of the benefits.

- *Spirituality*
  Spirituality is at the centre of healing and development. Connection with the Creator brings life, unity and love and purpose to the process, and is expressed through a heart-centred approach to all that we do.

- *Harmonising with natural law*
  Growth is a process of uncovering who we truly are as human beings in harmony with the natural laws of the universe.
- *Walking in balance*
  Codes of morality, ethics and protocol teach us how to walk the road of life in a good way. Violating moral and ethical boundaries can destroy the process of healing and development.
- *Working from principle*
  Our plans and actions are founded on our deepest understanding of the principles that describe how the universe is ordered, and how healing and development unfold.
- *Learning*
  Learning to live in ways that promote life and health is the essence of our development. Our primary strategy is therefore the promotion of this type of learning.
- *Sustainability*
  When we take actions to improve our lives or the lives of others, it is critical to avoid undermining the natural systems upon which all life depends, and to work in ways that enhance the capacity of people to continue in their own healing and development.
- *Move to the positive*
  Solving the critical problems in our lives and communities is best approached by visualising and moving into the positive alternatives that we wish to create, and building on the strengths we already have, rather than throwing away our energy fighting the negatives.
- *Be the change you want to see*
  In all of our actions, we seek to be living examples of the changes we wish to see in the world. By walking that path, we make the path visible.

With the courage and dedication to utilise the wisdom of our elders on the path to a peaceful and equitable future, we will find that we have the power and ability to carefully and lovingly remove any barriers that have limited the development of our full potential as human beings. The greater the difficulty in our path, the greater the opportunity for our growth and ultimate victory; we can become more than we have ever been.

We know from our ancient teachings that the sacred eagle of humanity has two perfectly balanced and harmonious wings; one representing woman, and one representing man. In our relationships as women and men, brothers and sisters, mothers and fathers, we must join together to eliminate all forms of disrespect, mistreatment, or lack of sharing in the responsibility of raising the world's children. It is my deepest prayer that with every new sunrise, we can recognise more and more that the most sacred and holy of all the wonderful ceremonies and gifts that the Creator has given us is the birth of a child, and that everything we can do to provide our children and communities the best possible future is a sacred gift and responsibility.

For is not the moment long, long overdue, my beloved relatives, through the unfailing power and love of our good Creator, for us to free ourselves completely from the hurt of both the past and present so we may truly soar like an eagle to the promised greatness of our sacred destiny and future?

Eagle Poem

To pray you open your whole self
To sky, to earth, to sun, to moon
To one whole voice that is you.
And know there is more
That you can't see, can't hear,
Can't know except in moments
Steadily growing, and languages
That aren't always sound but other
Circles of motion.
Like eagles that Sunday morning
Over Salt River. Circled in blue sky
In wind, swept our hearts clean
With sacred wings.
We see you, see ourselves and know
That we must take the utmost care
And kindness in all things.
Breath in, knowing we are made of
All this, and breathe, knowing
We are truely blessed because we
Were born, and die soon within a
True circle of motion,
Like eagles rounding out the morning
Inside us.
We pray that it will be done
In beauty.
In beauty.

Joy Harjo

About the Artists

El Anatsui (Ghana/Nigeria)
El Anatsui was born in the mid-1940s in Anyako, Ghana. He graduated from the College of Art, University of Science and Technology in Kumasi, majoring in sculpture. He works principally in wood, a medium that very effectively carries the bold vital force and strength of traditional African sculpture. His work has been exhibited throughout Africa, Europe and North America. He is now working in the Fine Arts department at the University of Nigeria.

Owusu Ankomah (Germany/Ghana)
Born in Sekondi, Ghana, in 1956, Owusu Ankomah was a student at the College of Art in Accra from 1971–74 before visiting Europe, working closely with a number of other artists, and running seminars on African Art. He has had solo exhibitions since 1971 and has been exhibiting his work in group shows since 1981. His work revolves around the human physique and he is fascinated by its strength and beauty. He now lives and works in Germany.

Victor Anicet (Martinique)
Victor Anicet was born in Marigot in 1938 and studied ceramics in France, England and Germany. He has always had an abiding interest in Amerindian art and this interest is a strong feature of his paintings and ceramic work. In 1984, together with a group of other artists, he formed the FWOMAJE group. He has exhibited alone, with this group and in other group shows; most recently in the USA, the Caribbean, France and Canada. Since 1967, he has taught in various lycees and colleges and at the Ecole Regionale d'Arts Plastiques. Since 1991 he has also run a ceramics studio at Riviere-Salee.

Ansupati (Indonesia)
Ansupati was born in 1957 and studied in Yogyakarta, Central Java, where he teaches today. He was awarded a scholarship to study at the School of Art and Design in New York. He usually chooses traditional items of practical use as motifs for his sculptures. Whether he works with stone, wood or metal, his objects also have a spiritual dimension. He experiments all the time with new materials – for example with different kinds of wood from his area. The process of creation means as much to Anusapati as the completed work.

Youssouf Bath (Ivory Coast)
Youssouf Bath was born in 1949 and currently teaches art in Abidjan. His work has been exhibited in the USA, Canada and France. He paints primarily on tree bark with colours he makes from leaves, fruit and earth. His paintings impart a mystical vision to scenes of everyday African life. Bath was chosen by UNESCO and the Cité de la Creation to represent black Africa in an international exhibition at the Musée Urbain Tony Garnier in Lyon, France, for his study of the Cité Ideale; this can now been seen as a fresco in the town itself. His works contain symbols, often animist in nature, evoking the creation of man, his traditional skills, his spiritual relations, the magic of beings and places.

Ricardo Benaim (Venezuela)
Ricardo Benaim was born in Caracas in 1949. He graduated from the Neuman Foundation Institute of Design in Caracas in 1972. He studied printmaking in Paris and lectured in New York. He now lives in Caracas. Since 1991, he has carried out a series of group activities where art and ecology are integrated. His current project is Un Marco por la Tiera, a programme of exhibitions to be shown throughout the Americas, containing the works of a group of artists, using art as a front of action to raise awareness, inform and sensitise the community about the environment.

Handan Borutecene (Turkey)
Handan Borutecene was born in Istanbul, Turkey in 1957. She studied art in both Istanbul and Paris and also took part in archeological excavations as well as working with sculpture and ceramics. Borutecene's sculptures use stone, metals, glass and plant materials to communicate her message, influenced no doubt through work in archeology, of the importance of not losing touch with nature or with each other. The materials used by the artist have existed since ancient times and symbolise the need not to forget our links with the past traditions and civilisations.

Alexander Borodie (Ukraine)
Alexander Borodie was born in 1946 in Dnipropetrovsk, where he started his studies at the Academy of Arts before continuing at the Academy of Arts in Kiev. In 1975 he became a member of the Ukrainian Artists Federation. During his studies, Borodie experimented with different artistic techniques, but he is mainly fascinated with working with enamel because of its plasticity and its vibrant colours. He rediscovered this old technique, known already in ancient Egypt, for genre-painting. This technique also has its tradition in Ukraine, and tradition plays an important role for Borodie, who tries to find a synthesis between the past and the present in his work. He wants to keep memories alive and revive forgotten but still vivid images and symbols.

Willem Boshoff (South Africa)
Willem Boshoff was born in 1951 in Vanderbijlpark. He obtained a National Art Teacher's Diploma in 1974 from the then Johannesburg College of Art, followed by a Higher Diploma in Fine Art in 1980 and a Masters Diploma in Technology in Fine Art in 1984. He has taught art since 1975, and his work is held in a number of public collections. As an artist he uses different media to reflect the situation in his country: seeds to represent hope and untapped creative forces, and medicine bottles to represent healing and alchemy. His approach is often original, challenging and memorable – such as a recent sculpture exhibition designed for a non-sighted public, where sighted visitors were not permitted to touch – emphasising the limitations of the more traditional artistic experience for this audience. He is married with three children.

Anahi Caceres (Argentina)
Born in Cordoba in 1953, Anahi Caceres is a prolific artist who, since 1972, has participated in over 300 group and 19 solo exhibitions, and 87 private and public art shows in Argentina, Chile, Spain, Puerto Rico, Brazil, Venezuela, Colombia, France and the USA. Her work (paintings, drawings, engravings, sculpture and installations) may be seen as belonging broadly to the 'anthropological' school and have a timeless quality. She has won a number of awards for her work.

Maria Teresa Cano (Colombia)
Maria Teresa Cano, born in Medellin in 1960, uses everyday materials, such as sugar, paraffin, cutlery and plates in her work. These are used both as domestic symbols and as reference points for metaphors about the role of women, a dominant theme in her work. Since graduating from the Universidad de Antioquia in Medellin in 1989, she has taught painting, illustration and other courses at several Columbian universities. She has exhibited mainly in Colombia, though her work has also been shown in group exhibitions in Holland, England, France, Venezuela, the USA, Brazil, Switzerland, Puerto Rico and Mexico.

Tony Capellan (Dominican Republic)
Tony Capellan was born in Tamboril in 1955 and studied Fine Art at Santo Domingo University. Since 1979 he has exhibited all over Central and South America, the USA and Europe, most recently in Holland, Mexico and Florida, as well as the Dominican Republic. He has received many prizes over the years and his work is in a number of collections worldwide. He uses everyday objects (children's shirts, chairs, plates, cases, lamps) and a variety of materials (wood, metal, water, glass, canvas and cloth) to produce memorable images in the form of installations and wall hangings.

Rimar Cardillo (Uruguay/USA)
Rimar Cardillo was born in Uruguay in 1944, but currently resides in New York. He began his artistic education in 1968 at the National School of Fine Arts and then moved to Germany, where he studied at the Zowessensee School of Art and Architecture in Berlin. He completed his education at the Leipzig School of Graphic Arts in 1971. He has mounted many solo exhibitions and taken part in numerous group shows. His works are sculptural and include many objects found in nature. They incorporate the cultural history of the native peoples of Latin America. His style has a confrontational attitude towards the destruction of nature and the disappearance of traditions and memory.

Nike Olanigi Davies (Nigeria)
Nike Davies, born in 1951 near Oshogbo, is one of the leading exponents of the art of batik, which has a long tradition among the Yoruba tribe in West Nigeria. The ideas for her paintings on fabric derive from old story telling as well as from personal experiences and memories. Traditional production and use of material are predominant, but her newly developed fixing technique with wax increases the brilliance of the colours. For Nike Davies, art always carries a message, and the foundation of the Nike Centre of Art and Culture in Oshogbo offers her and pupils from around the world a forum for learning and exchange. It is here where she teaches the origins and sources of her artistic style and promotes cultural exchange.

Buu Chi (Vietnam)
A self-proclaimed humanist, Buu Chi became involved with the anti-war movement while a law student at Hue University. After graduating in 1971, he was arrested and imprisoned by the Republic of Vietnam for his activities. The horrors he saw and experienced in prison have had a powerful influence on his work. Buu Chi understands the misery of the imprisoned — even after he was freed in 1975, the loss of time and space he experienced became his major concern. A self-taught artist, he used his talent to release his anguish and his feelings of pessimism are gradually lifting. Before beauty, Buu Chi feels an artist should express reality in his work. The sun, moon and clock faces are potent symbols of fleeting time. Despondent, haggard or pensive figures populate his work. In 1988 he spent some time in Paris, following his one-man exhibition there, and his work has since gained greater renown.

Duck-Hyun Cho (Korea)
Duck-Hyun Cho, born in 1957, is a professor of Fine Art at Hansung University. He studied at Seoul National University and has exhibited in Germany, France, Poland, the USA, Chile, Japan and Korea. His detailed paintings, particularly in the two series Site-Memory of the 20th Century and A History of Korean Women, use representational images of recent Korean history — concentrating on war and women — to explore the relationship between past and present. He employs framing devices to emphasise themes of containment and perception.

Rashid Diab (Sudan/Spain)
Rashid Diab is an accomplished painter and printmaker who was born in Wad Medani on the banks of the Blue Nile in Sudan in 1957. He now lives and works in Madrid, Spain, where he has owned and directed the Medani Galeria since the early 1980s. He is both an artist and a critic. He is a graduate of the Khartoum College of Fine Art and in 1980 travelled to Madrid on a scholarship from the goverment of Spain, where he completed several graduate degrees, culminating in a PhD in Fine Art at Complutense University in Madrid. He has received many awards and his works have been exhibited throughout the world.

Siron Franco (Brazil)
Siron Franco, born in 1947, lives in Goiania, Central Brazil. He started painting when he was twelve years old and to this day painting has remained the most important form of his artistic expression, alongside performance art, etching and sculpture. From the beginning, he has been preoccupied with the art of the indigenous people of Brazil. His Monument of the Indian Nations, created in 1992 for the Earth Summit in Rio, symbolises the variety and the wealth of the Indian culture, which he passionately wishes to preserve. In one of his collages he satirises the Brazilian flag by creating the flag's image using symbolising population growth and economic corruption.

Monica Gonzalez and Osvaldo Salerno (Paraguay)
A painter and sculptor, Monica Gonzalez was born in Asuncion in 1952. Over the last few years she has exhibited in Brazil, Peru and Germany, as well as in Paraguay, and she has received a number of awards. Since 1972 she has also been involved in teaching activities. Her time is divided between Art and family life (she has three children), and domestic objects also feature in her work.
Osvaldo Salerno was also born in 1952 and is an architect, engraver, painter and graphic designer. He studied in Paraguay, Spain and Argentina and is currently Founder-Director of the Museo del Barro. Outside Paraguay, his work is held in collections in Spain, Iran, Argentina, Brazil and Colombia.

Gongkar Gyatso (Tibet)
Born in Lhasa, Tibet, in 1961, Gongkar Gyatso the artist describes himself as 'a child of the Cultural Revolution'. As well as graduating from high school in Llasa, he also obtained a qualification in Chinese painting from the School of Fine Arts in Beijing in 1978, and then graduated from the Central Institute of Nationalities in 1984. In 1989 he spent a year at the Central Institute of Fine Arts and Crafts doing research. He has been exhibiting his work for the last ten years; the paintings seek the artistic roots of his own Tibetan heritage. He is now the resident graphics designer for the Library of Tibetan Work and Archives in Dharamsala, India.

Ariffin Mohd Ismail (Malaysia)
Ariffin Mohd Ismail was born in Malaysia in 1952. He has a diploma from the MARA Technology Institute and an MA from Manchester Polytechnic. His most recent work has been concerned with the political dimensions of the destruction of our environment. He hopes to raise awareness about who is in a position to solve the planet's problems, as well as to inspire love for it. He is currently lecturing in Fine Art at the Malaysian Islamic Academy of Science.

Angus Cockney Kaanerk (Canada)
A sculptor, Angus Cockney Kaanerk was born in 1957 in Tuktoyaktuk, and his Inuit background is clearly reflected in the squat, solid roundness of his art. At the age of eight, he left his home town and only returned relatively recently, in 1981. As a young man he competed as a cross-country skier and this enabled him to travel around the world. Visiting art galleries on his travels, he knew he wanted to carve and when he finally retired from skiing and returned to Tuktoyaktuk, he began to sculpt. His forms resemble the figures of animals and people carved as Inuit good luck charms, and his work is inspired by his peoples' myths and traditions.

Bogolan Kasobane Group (Mali)
This group was formed in 1978 and consists of six painters from the Institut National des Arts of Mali. Their work is broadly based in the Bogolan tradition, using established colours, tools and methods; but the artists distinguish themselves by their innovation in composition and the range of colours they employ, as well as by originality in the presentation of their work. They have exhibited in Mali and across the world; most recent international exhibitions were in Germany, France, Japan, Cuba and Burkina-Faso.

Hamiduzzaman Khan (Bangladesh)
In 1946 Khan was born into a Muslim family and on matriculation from Banagran High School in 1962 he gained admission to the Government Art College in Dhaka. Following an accident in 1969, he went to England for medical treatment where, inspired by the Art Galleries he visited, he began to sculpt. In 1970 he began teaching at the Institute of Fine Art and received a Masters Degree. At this point he participated in a number of group exhibitions and shows, in particular from 1980–85. Over this period his style has changed at least three times, but he has maintained the beauty of his work throughout.

Khalid Khreis (Jordan)
Born in Kerak, Jordan, in 1955, Khalid Khreis has studied art, drawing, painting and sculpture in a variety of Art Schools and Academies in Egypt, Spain, Italy, Mexico and Jordan. He is an established painter in his native Jordan and has exhibited throughout the world, most recently in England, Spain, France, Italy, Canada, UAE and Jordan. He has been a finalist in many international exhibitions and competitions and won awards for his work, which is principally abstract and conceptual.

Ivo Lill (Estonia)
The glass artist Ivo Lill was born in 1953 and studied at the School of Arts in Tallinn. In the tradition of the sculptor, he is both a craftsman and an artist. In his work he uses mirrors to strengthen the visual effect, the reflections and the transparency of the glass. His objects are fascinating because of the intense colours he is able to achieve by the use of special techniques. His recent pyramid work reflects the common struggle for peace of mind as a 'high point' in all our lives. His work has been exhibited in Russia, Japan and all over Europe.

Joseph Madisia (Namibia)
Joseph Madisia was born in Luderitz, southern Namibia, in 1954. He belongs to those artists who aim at a new understanding of art after the independence of Namibia. Political subjects such as unity, democracy, reconciliation, and equal rights for women are central elements of his work. Joseph Madisia also tries to stimulate ecological awareness by using materials such as cardboard, which do not alter the balance of nature. His work is represented in numerous private and public collections in Namibia, South Africa, UK, France, USA, Bangladesh, India, Switzerland, Norway and Germany.

Louise Metzger (Sierra Leone)
Born in Freetown, Louise Metzger obtained a Diploma in Art Education and from 1955–56 taught at St Joseph's Convent secondary school (where she had previously been a student) as head of the Art department. In 1962, she moved to Sierra Leone grammar school, later becoming principal lecturer and working in the Arts and Crafts department at Milton Margai. Subsequently she retired to set up her own studios: GAGA Studios. She has also been a part-time lecturer in Art Methods at Fourah Bay College. Her work has been exhibited in Britain, the USA and Sierra Leone and she recently mounted a solo exhibition of her work in London.

Johan Mhlanga (Swaziland)

Johan Mhlanga lives in a village in Swaziland. He earned a living for himself and his family as a cook before he became aware of his vocation as a woodcarver through a dream. Religion, intuition and a strong relationship with nature are important aspects in Johan Mhlanga's artistic creations. 'The wood tells me what it wants to be turned into', and so he gives the predestined form an expression. His sculptures bear a direct relationship with their environment and the prevailing life conditions. Johan Mhlanga considers his work as a contribution to the preservation of old traditions for future generations, as well as an occupation which gives life a meaning.

Steve Ngigi (Kenya)

A Gospel musician and music teacher, Steve Ngigi, born in Kiambu in 1952, graduated in music education from Kenyatta University in 1987. Since then he has divided his time between music, music teaching and sculpting. He has exhibited in Kenya and South Africa, producing both wood and stone sculpture, but works principally in wood. His work is concerned with social and environmental issues, such as pollution and the destruction of the environment. He is currently a lecturer at St Mary's College in Bura.

Santiago Olazabel (Cuba)

The work of Santiago Olazabel, born in Havana in 1955, has been very much influenced by the Afro-Cuban religious tradition *santeria*, which his family still practises. The spirituality and values of this element of the African heritage in contemporary Cuban culture is also evident in the work of other modern Cuban artists. Santiago Olazabel studied at the San Alejandro Academy of Art and has exhibited mainly in Cuba, but his work has also been included in group exhibitions in many Latin American and European countries, most recently in Turkey, Brazil, Spain, Hungary and Italy.

One World Quilt Group (UK)

The Group, founded in Milton Keynes just prior to the Earth Summit in 1992, have set themselves the target to create awareness of the commonality of life for women all over the world. Using traditional 'female skills' such as sewing, embroidery, making bobbin-lace or knitting they produced a patchwork blanket. The conditions of life, the problems and needs of women in the Third World are central themes of the individual pieces. They created a kaleidoscope of messages, opinions, ideas and feelings about a more understanding and respectful way of dealing with different cultures and issues.

Cecilia Martner Peyrelongue (Chile/Mexico)

This artist was born in Chile in 1956, but has been exhibiting her work in Chile and Mexico in group shows since 1979, and in solo exhibitions since 1988. She has studied extensively, following a number of courses since 1975: architecture, teaching, drawing, engraving, painting and, in particular, stained-glass, in both Mexico and Chile. She has taught art at various levels in a number of schools and institutes, but in recent years has concentrated on teaching and working with stained-glass. Working from her own studio, she has produced around 40 pieces for windows, doors and walls in churches, restaurants, gardens and commercial centres.

Marilene Phipps (Haiti/USA)

Marilene Phipps was born in Haiti in 1951. She studied at the University of Pennsylvania and also did undergraduate work in anthropology. Her images, she says, are drawn from the 'visual excitement of childhood'. They are of people 'magically' connected with their environment. She hopes her paintings can be experienced on three levels. Firstly as 'sensuous, textured, abstract colour'. Secondly, as raising issues of psychological consequence. She speaks a metaphorical language using elements of physical life for words. Finally, all her work relates to Haitian myth: she uses the symbolism of her ancient voodoo religion. She now lives in the USA and is a fellow at Harvard University.

Marko Pogacnik (Slovenia)

Marko Pogacnik, born in 1944 in Kranj, studied at the Academy of Fine Arts in Ljubljana. From 1966–70 he was a member of the artists group 'OHO', which dealt with conceptual and 'landscape art'. He lives in Sempas, in the Vipava valley, close to the Italian border. The threat to the ecological system of the planet is his central theme. He wants to reconcile man and nature. Since 1986 he has worked periodically on a series of sculptures, 'Heal the Earth'. Wherever he works he invites local people to his workshops to make this work come alive for the community.

Nestor Quinones (Mexico)
Nestor Quinones is a self-taught artist who was born in Mexico City in 1967. He has had three solo shows in Mexico City, but has also exhibited widely in group exhibitions. In recent years his work has been seen in the USA, Belgium, Germany, Spain and Mexico. Working on collective projects with a group of artists at his home, La Quinonera, over the last seven years they have organised independent exhibitions together and developed a dynamic working relationship in which individual creativity is contained within, but not stifled by, the requirements of the group.

Movimiento Manuela Ramos (Peru)
The 'Creative Women's Workshop', part of the Manuela Ramos Movement based in Lima, grew out of the production of posters, postcards and magazines for a campaign about domestic violence in 1983. This led to a recognition of the creative potential of the women involved and the possibility of generating income from artistic endeavours. They use their needlework skills on squares of material to produce arpilleria (appliqué) artwork. At present the workshop consists of 11 women from the popular barrios districts, north and south of Lima, working together in the evenings when they are free from other community and domestic activities.

Osmo Rauhala (Finland)
Osmo Rauhala studied at the Free Arts School and the Academy of Arts in Helsinki, as well as at the School of Visual Arts in New York. In 1992, he was elected 'Young Artist of the Year' in Finland. From May to October he lives in the countryside, and his life is shaped by being a farmer in summer and an artist in winter. He believes that farming and art have a lot in common and the wildlife of the countryside is the inspiration for his artistic work. In his words, 'the element of the interaction between man and nature is whether language and the concepts we have created can describe the system we are dependent on.'

Efrain Recinos (Guatemala)
A civil engineering graduate of San Carlos University, Efrain Recinos, who was born in 1928, has also studied design in England and acoustics in Denmark. A painter and sculptor, he is also an architect and attempts to integrate these different disciplines in his work; this can be seen most clearly in the Cultural Centre of Guatemala. He has been exhibiting since 1963, and has received a number of prizes, among them the 'Opus Especial' for the design of the National Theatre. His paintings exude peace and humour and his sculpture uses waste materials discarded by contemporary society.

Laila Shawa (Palestine/UK)
Laila Shawa was born in 1940 in Gaza, Palestine and has studied art in Palestine, Egypt, Italy and Austria. Having worked as a professional painter, illustrator of children's books and stained-glass worker, she now lives and works in London. Shawa's work is deeply linked with her roots in Gaza, often using calligraphy, in the form of graffiti rather than decoration, to put across both the violent and humane content of her message. Shawa uses the medium of photography for its immediacy and silk screening to incorporate geometric shapes and bold primary colours into the images of graffitied walls. Shawa feels that to chronicle one's times is an artist's duty.

Gizella Varga Sinai (Iran/Hungary)
Gizella Varga Sinai, born in Hungary, lived in Vienna before she moved to Iran in 1967. In her early years she was already fascinated by art, but it was only in Iran that she took up painting. Her paintings are partly expressions of events in her childhood and memories of her homeland. Gizella Varga Sinai does not follow a particular style. Her spectrum includes expressionist paintings as well as traditional Persian painting. She studied at Vienna's Akademie fur Angewandte Kunst. Gizella Varga Sinai's work has been exhibited in Iran, Pakistan, Europe and Canada.

Gazbia Sirry (Egypt)
Gazbia Sirry was born into an intellectual family in Cairo and after high school began studying at the Fine Art College in Cairo. She then moved to Paris to work in the studios of Marcel Gromaire. Her studies continued in Italy and then as a postgraduate at the Slade school in London from 1954–55. Over the years, her style has developed from distinctly Egyptian to being more expressionistic. She works in multi media and her paintings consist of layers of colour and form. She has a strong emotional attachment to her work, which is dedicated both to her husband and her love of life.

Vivan Sundaram (India)
Vivan Sundaram was born in 1943 in Simla, in the north of India. He studied in Baroda. Today he lives and works in Delhi and is counted among the most famous artists of his country. For his installations, Vivan Sundaram often works with a number of other artists and craftsmen, using different kinds of materials, such as steel, marble insets and painted objects to produce artwork which creates a powerful effect on the viewer by means of careful composition. His work usually has a precise social or political context, and he has been particularly concerned about tensions between Hindus and Muslims in recent years.

Kimio Tsuchiya (Japan)
Born in 1955 in Fukui, Kimio Tsuchiya studied in the Architecture Department at Nihon University, graduating in 1977, and in 1988 attended the MA sculpture course at Chelsea School of Art in London. He has exhibited in Europe, particularly England and France, as well as in the USA and Japan. He works in stone, metal and wood, often using old furniture or materials salvaged from buildings, or driftwood rescued from the sea or rivers. His powerful sculpture is usually large scale, whether it is for exhibition in the midst of the countryside or, more conventionally, in a gallery.

Judy Watson and Gonzalo Mella (Australia/Chile)
Judy Watson was born in 1959 in Mundubbera, Queensland. Her artwork over the past 10 years has been concerned with social issues, particularly feminism, racial history and cultural displacement. She is a direct desendent of the Waanyi clan. Besides exhibiting internationally, she has formed artists cooperatives in Australia, and also helps acccss facilities for isolated artists.
Gonzalo Mella was born in Valparaiso, Chile and has exhibited his work on Chile and in Australia where he now lives. His work is rooted in his heritage and the history of the Americas.

Cecilia Martner Peyrelongue (Chile)
This artist was born in Chile in 1956, but has been exhibiting her work in Chile and Mexico in group shows since 1979, and in solo exhibitions since 1988. She has studied extensively, following a number of courses since 1975: architecture, teaching, drawing, engraving, painting and, in particular, stained-glass, in both Mexico and Chile. She has taught art at various levels in a number of schools and institutes, but in recent years has concentrated on teaching and working with stained-glass. Working from her own studio, she has produced around 40 pieces for windows, doors and walls in churches, restaurants, gardens and commercial centres.

Yang Yanping and Zeng Shanqing (China)
Zeng Shanqing, born in 1932 in Beijing, is a well-known contemporary figure painter who trained at the Central Academy of Fine Arts in Beijing. He has exhibited widely in the Far East, the United States, and now Europe. His paintings portray themes drawn from China's minority peoples and animal forms, with a vigorous use of ink and strong colours. He has been living and working in New York State since 1986 with his wife Yang Yanping.
Yang Yanping, born in Nanjng in 1934, is one of the most innovative of contemporary Chinese painters using ink and oils. She graduated from Qinghua University in Beijing with a degree in architecture, initially taught industrial design and then created historical paintings from the Museum of Chinese History. In 1980 her status as a leading artist was confirmed when she joined the prestigious Beijing Painting Academy. In 1986, she moved to the United States and began a long association with the State University of New York. Yang's personal symbol is the lotus plant, the Chinese symbol of purity, which she reinterprets in semi-abstract compositions of ethereal beauty. Her works have been exhibited internationally.

Zerihun Yetmgeta (Ethiopia)
Zerihun Yetmgeta was born in Addia Ababa in 1941, but considers himself an international artist. His talent was evident at an early age; he always enjoyed working with his hands. Three artists in particular have influenced him: two of his teachers at the School of Fine Art, and Skunder, with whom he shared a studio in the mid-eighties. He works in mixed media on bamboo strips and enjoys the use of colour in his paintings, which he considers typical of the Ethiopian style of church paintings.

Gladman Zinyeka (Zimbabwe)
Gladman Zinyeka was born in 1962 in the Gutu district. Today he lives in Chitungwiza, 30 km outside Harare. He works in the 'Gallery 2000', a setting where works by local sculptors are exhibited in a natural environment. His works deal with the relationship between man and woman but also with emotions and their meaning for thinking and acting in daily life. Gladman Zinyeka hopes his work is a voice for universal suffering and sees sharing the expression of pain as a means of unifying and strengthening.

About the Authors

Anil Agarwal
Director of the Centre for Science and Environment in New Delhi, India, Anil Agarwal started his career as a science correspondent. He then worked at Earthscan, London where he produced numerous reports and publications. He set up the Centre for Science and Environment which has played a key role in the growth of environmental awareness in India. He also edits the *Down to Earth* magazine, which provides a Southern perspective to major environmental events. Mr Agarwal is a member of several government committees on policy issues. He has received many prestigious awards such as the UNEP 500 Roll of Honour.

Alicia Barcena
Alicia Barcena is an ecologist and is the Executive Director of Earth Council, Costa Rica. She was Principal Officer on Oceans, Coastal and Development and Living Alicia Barcena Marine Resources, UNCED, from 1990 to 1992 and General Director at the National Institute of Fisheries in Mexico from 1988 to 1990. Her publications include *Programa Nacional de Ecologia, Comision Nacional de Ecologia, Programas de Trabajo (21 Aciones)*, and *Prevencion y Control de Contaminacion (Agua, Aire y Suelo)*.

Adrian Cleasby
Adrian Cleasby studied philosophy at St Andrews University, Edinburgh, and now works on behalf of the UK's leading development, environment and human rights NGOs as Project Coordinator of 3WE – The Third World and Environment Broadcasting Project. 3WE is a research and lobby outfit which puts the case for sustained, imaginative and fair representation of global affairs in the mass media.

Javier Pérez de Cuéllar
President of the World Commission on Culture and Development (UNESCO, Paris), his Excellency Pérez de Cuéllar was Secretary-General of the United Nations from 1982–1991. He is now President of the International Disability Foundation (Geneva), and in 1993 became President of the Fondation de l'Arche de la Fraternité (Paris). Born in Peru in 1920, Mr Perez de Cuellar is the author of *Manual de Derecho Diplomatico* (1964) and *Anarchy or Order* (1992). He is married, with two children.

Susan George
Susan George, born in the US and now a US-French citizen living in Paris, is Associate Director of the Transnational Institute in Amsterdam. She holds degrees from Smith College, the Sorbonne and the Ecole des Hautes Etudes en Sciences Sociales. The most recent of her eight books on North-South issues is *Faith and Credit: the World Bank's Secular Empire* (with Fabrizio Sabelli); other titles include *How the Other Half Dies: the Real Reasons for World Hunger; A Fate Worse than Debt; Ill Fares the Land* (Penguin) and *The Debt Boomerang* (Pluto Press). Her work has been translated into a dozen languages.

Dr Saad Eddin Ibrahim
Dr Ibrahim is a leading intellectual in the Arab world. Born and educated in Egypt, he concluded his studies in Cairo University, UCLA and the University of Washington. He is chairman of the board of the Ibn Khaldoun Center for Development Studies and Professor of Political Sociology at the American University in Cairo. He is also a member of the Club of Rome, an adviser to the World Bank on environmentally sustainable development, and the author of numerous articles and books.

Phil Lane
Phil Lane was born in Lawrence, Kansas, where his mother and father met attending Haskell Indian School. He is an enrolled member of the Yankton Sioux and Chickasaw Tribes and a traditionally recognised hereditary chief. During the past 26 years he has worked with indigenous people in North and South America, Micronesia, Thailand, Hawaii and Africa. He is currently an Associate Professor, and International Coordinator of the Four Worlds Institute for Human and Community Development at the University of Lethbridge in Alberta, Canada. The Institute is internationally recognised for its work in human and community transformation because of its unique focus on the importance of spirituality and culture in development.

Joy Harjo
Born in Tulsa, Oklahoma in 1951, Joy Harjo is an enrolled member of the Muscogee (or Creek) Tribe. She has published five books of poetry including *She Had Some Horses*, and the award winning *In Mad Love and War*. She is currently on leave from her post as Professor in the creative writing program at the University of New Mexico. She is also a dramatic screenwriter and is working on an original screenplay *When We Used To Be Humans* for the American Film Foundation. Ms Harjo plays saxophone with her band, *Poetic Justice*, which will soon be releasing a CD.

Wangari Maathai
Professor Wangari Maathai is the winner of the Africa Award and founder of the Green Belt Movement, Nairobi. She was born in 1940 to a farming family. In 1960 she won a scholarship to an American college, followed by university, and returned to Nairobi to take her doctorate. Maathai has been a devoted environmentalist since 1974 when, as an anatomy lecturer at Nairobi University, the National Council of Women invited her to lead their fight against poverty. Her renowned work has brought considerable personal hardship, including imprisonment.

Mary Midgley
Mary Midgley, born in 1919, formerly lecturer in philosophy at the University of Newcastle upon Tyne, is a philosopher with a special interest in moral evolution, the environment and the uses of science. Books include *Beast and Man; Animals and Why They Matter; Wickedness* and *The Ethical Primate*. Mary Midgley is married to another philosopher, Geoffrey Midgley, has three sons, and lives in Newcastle upon Tyne.

Njabulo Ndebele
Njabulo Ndebele grew up in Western Native Township in Johannesburg, South Africa, and later in Charterston Location, Nigel. He holds a BA degree in English and Philosophy from the National University of Lesotho (1973); an MA from Cambridge University (1978); and a Doctorate in Philosophy from the University of Denver (1983). Professor Ndebele is the Vice Chancellor and Principal at the University of the North, the largest historically black university in South Africa. He holds membership to a number of outside bodies including the Research Chairmanship of the Committee of University Principals, is a Board Member of the SABC, The Joint Education Trust, The Centre for Science Development, the Education Committee of The Urban Foundation. He is President of the National Arts Coalition and President of the Congress of South African Writers. Described as 'a prophet of the post-apartheid condition', Professor Ndebele is a prize-winning author, poet and critic, and one of the leading lights in South Africa's literacy world.

Shridath Ramphal
Sir Shridath Ramphal is Co-Chairman of the Commission on Global Governance. He was the Secretary-General of the Commonwealth from 1975–1990 and earlier Minister of Foreign Affairs and of Justice of Guyana. He served on each of the independent commissions which reported on global issues in the 1980s, chaired the West Indian Commission, and is a member of the Carnegie Commission on Preventing Deadly Conflict. President of the World Conservation Union – IUCN 1990-93, he is now President of LEAD International, a programme to promote Leadership in Environment and Development. His book *Our Country The Planet* was written for the Earth Summit. He is Chancellor of the University of the West Indies and of the University of Warwick in Britain, a member of the Board of Canada's International Development Research Centre (IDRC) and of the Council of the International Negotiating Network set up by former US President Jimmy Carter.

Nafis Sadik
Dr Nafis Sadik is Executive Director of the United Nations Population Fund (UNFPA) and holds the rank of Under-Secretary General. On her appointment in 1987, she became the first woman to head one of the United Nations' major voluntary-funded programmes. In 1994, she served as Secretary-General of the International Conference on Population and Development. A Pakistani national and a physician, Dr Sadik is a former Director-General of Pakistan's Central Family Planning Council. She is the recipient of numerous awards and honorary degrees, and in 1988 was elected to the Fellowship *ad eundem* of the Royal College of Obstetricians and Gynaecologists of the United Kingdom. She has written numerous articles, and edited three books, on family planning, health and development. UNFPA, with a staff of 800, is the world's largest source of multilateral support to population programmes, providing assistance in over 140 countries and territories.

Vandana Shiva
Dr Vandana Shiva is Director of the Research Foundation for Science, Technology and Natural Resource Policy, Dehra Dun, India, and also Director of Navdanya, a seed conservation project. She is an advisor to the Third World Network in Penang and consultant to the FAO in New Delhi. Her publications include: *Monocultures of the Mind; Sustaining Diversity; Women, Ecology and Health; Ecology and the Politics of Survival;* and *Staying Alive: Women, Ecology and Survival in India*. Dr Shiva is Visiting Professor at Schumacher College, England, and the University of Oslo, Norway.

Catherine Thick
Catherine Thick studied philosophy, anthropology and politics. During the 1980s, she was a consultant in management and fundraising to the boards of several charities in health, culture and ecology. Catherine travelled widely and her study of art practices around the world not only influenced her own painting but also raised her concern about the relationship between environmental and cultural diversity, both increasingly under threat. She then began to question more seriously the direction of the development models being promoted in, particularly, Asia, Africa and Latin America. In 1986, she started to pursue the idea of an international art project to help inspire a spiritual and cultural dimension to the 'sustainable development' debate, which became established in 1990 having secured the support of several non-governmental organizations and UNESCO. Catherine is now Director of *The Right to Hope* Trust, founded in South Africa in 1995.

Desmond Mlipo Tutu
Born in 1931 in South Africa, The Most Reverend Desmond Tutu is the Archbishop of Cape Town. He holds over thirty honorary degrees from academic institutions in Europe and the United States. His work against poverty and oppression is known worldwide; among other awards, Reverend Tutu received the Nobel Peace Prize in 1984 for his work against apartheid. He has written many articles and several books of which *The Rainbow People* is his most recent publication.

The Right to Hope Trust
Societe Generale House
30 Wellington Rd
Parktown 2193
Johannesburg
South Africa
Fax: +27 11 484 2650

One World Support UK
2 Ferdinand Place
London
UK
NW1 8EE
Fax: +44 171 284 3374